# EVIDENCE

"*Oneing*" is an old English word that was used by Lady Julian of Norwich (1342–1416) to describe the encounter between God and the soul. The Center for Action and Contemplation proudly borrows the word to express the divine unity that stands behind all of the divisions, dichotomies, and dualisms in the world. We pray and publish with Jesus' words, "that all may be one" (John 17:21).

EDITOR:

Vanessa Guerin

PUBLISHER:

The Center for Action and Contemplation

ADVISORY BOARD:

David Benner
James Danaher
Ilia Delio, OSF
Sheryl Fullerton
Marion Küstenmacher

Design and Composition by Nelson Kane Design

Hebrews 11:1 in Greek calligraphy by Georgia Angelopoulos

# Oneing

VOLUME 2 NO. 2

# EDITOR'S NOTE

A T THE END of *Portrait of a Radical: The Jesus Movement,*[1] Fr. Richard Rohr says, "faith is rare...[which is] why Jesus himself said, '...when [he] returns, will he find any faith on the earth?' (Lk 18:8)." Fr. Richard concludes, "I think Jesus really had doubts."

And why wouldn't Jesus have doubts? "Since the Enlightenment we have become more and more situated in a world of our own making, with cyberspace being the emblematic example of the moment.... The demand is put on faith to be effective, experiential, and relevant," writes Mark Muldoon in "The Perils of Spiritual Faith, Doubt, and Evidence." Much of the world is consumed with and distracted by a desire for increasing validation through technology and social media, rather than trust in what "St. Bonaventure, Teilhard de Chardin, many poets, and everyday mystics found...in the natural world, in elements, seasons, animals, and all living things," as Fr. Richard writes in his introduction to this edition of *Oneing.*

"This is why an *evidential* worldview has become crucial," emphasizes Michael Dowd in his article on evidential mysticism. "We now know that evolutionary and ecological processes are at the root of life and human culture. To disregard, to dishonor, these processes through our own determined ignorance and cultural/religious self-focus is an evil that will bring untold suffering to countless generations, of our own kind and of all our relations. We must denounce such a legacy. Ours is thus a call to action—a call to sacred activism."

We often see this call to action through art, which in itself is a form of sacred activism. Twentieth-century Abstract Expressionist

Mark Rothko's veiled paintings, in their mysterious, evidential nature, have served as a lure for viewers who recognize that, in the paintings' presence, they are entering into a sacred space. Many, including myself, have indeed experienced a reverential awe in the Rothko Room at The Phillips Collection in Washington, D.C., and in Houston's more contemplative Rothko Chapel. I personally have a renewed interest in spending time in the chapel, thanks to these words from Susan J. Barnes' article in this edition of *Oneing*: "The Rothko Chapel…quickly became a pioneering institution honoring human rights and a distinguished, visionary center hosting inter-religious dialogue, including international colloquia, as well as a place where individuals come to meditate and congregations of many different faiths are welcomed to worship."

The contributors to this superb edition of *Oneing* give abundant evidence of Presence within and around everything that exists. "The fundamental fact of existence is that this trust in God, this faith, is the firm foundation under everything that makes life worth living. It's our handle on what we can't see" (Heb 11:1).[2] I believe these authors give us an opportunity to re-energize our faith through the evidence of "13.8 billion years of divine creativity," as Michael Dowd says so beautifully. With evidence like this, there is a good possibility that when Jesus returns, his doubts might well prove unsubstantiated.

Vanessa Guerin,
*Editor*

# CONTRIBUTORS

RICHARD ROHR, OFM, is a Franciscan of the New Mexico Province and the Founding Director of the Center for Action and Contemplation (CAC) in Albuquerque, New Mexico. An internationally-recognized author and spiritual leader, Father Richard teaches primarily on incarnational mysticism, non-dual consciousness, and contemplation, with a particular emphasis on how these affect the social justice issues of our time. Along with many recorded conferences, he is the author of numerous books, including the newly-released *Eager to Love: The Alternative Way of Francis of Assisi* and *Dancing Standing Still: Healing the World from a Place of Prayer*, an updated edition of *A Lever and a Place to Stand*. To learn more about Father Richard Rohr and the CAC, visit cac.org.

THE REV. MICHAEL DOWD M.DIV., is an evidential mystic, eco-theologian, and bestselling author whose work has been featured in *The New York Times, Los Angeles Times, Wall Street Journal, Washington Post, Newsweek, Discover,* and on CNN, ABC News, and Fox News. His 2009 book, *Thank God for Evolution*, was endorsed by six Nobel laureates and by religious leaders across the spectrum. Michael and his science-writer wife, Connie Barlow, have addressed some 2,000 groups across North America since 2002. Their passion is showing how a sacred-science view of reality can inspire people of diverse backgrounds and beliefs to work together in service to a just and thriving future for all. To learn more about the Rev. Michael Dowd, visit TheGreatStory.org or MichaelDowd.org.

MARK S. MULDOON, PHD, is currently the executive director of an organization that houses youth who are at risk of becoming homeless. Originally trained as a forester, he received his doctorate from the Catholic University of Louvain. He has taught in several post-secondary institutions while publishing widely in philosophy and spirituality, particularly with regard to phenomenology and the ideas of Paul Ricœur. He is the author of books, essays, and short stories. "The Addicted Pilgrim" appeared in *Presence: An International Journal of Spiritual Direction* in June 2014. To learn more about Mark Muldoon, visit wayfarer1.brinkster.net.

JAMES FINLEY, PhD, lived as a monk at the cloistered Trappist monastery of the Abbey of Gethsemani in Kentucky, where the world-renowned monk and author, Thomas Merton, was his spiritual director. A clinical psychologist in private practice, a retreat and workshop leader, and a member of the core faculty of the CAC's Living School for Action and Contemplation, James Finley is the author of *Merton's Palace of Nowhere, The Contemplative Heart,* and *Christian Meditation: Experiencing the Presence of God.* To learn more about James Finley, visit www.ContemplativeWay.org.

THE REV. CYNTHIA BOURGEAULT, PhD, is a modern day mystic, Episcopal priest, writer, and internationally recognized retreat leader. Cynthia divides her time between solitude at her seaside hermitage in Maine and a demanding schedule traveling globally to teach and spread the recovery of the Christian Contemplative and Wisdom paths. She is the founding director of both The Contemplative Society and the Aspen Wisdom School. A member of the core faculty of the CAC's Living School for Action and Contemplation, Cynthia is the author of eight books, including *The Holy Trinity and the Law of Three.* To learn more about Cynthia Bourgeault, visit www.contemplative.org/cynthia.html.

THE REV. SUSAN J. BARNES PhD, was a young member of the Rice University Museum staff, working for Dominique de Menil, when the Rothko Chapel was built. Called to the priesthood from her art-museum career, she was ordained in 2001. She is Rector of St. John's Episcopal Church in Minneapolis. To learn more about the Rev. Susan J. Barnes, visit www.stjohns-mpls.org/on-sundays/about-clergy.

CRAIG M. NELSON, PhD, CLS, a clinical ethicist and the Medical Bioethics Director for Kaiser Permanente South Bay Medical Center in Harbor City, California, has also been a lecturer at California State University, Fullerton, in the Departments of Comparative Religion and Liberal Studies. He was a recipient of the 2001 Science and Religion Course Award from the John Templeton Foundation and Center for Theology and Natural Science and has presented at recent American Society of Bioethics and Humanities annual meetings. His written work includes publications in science, religion, and ethics. Craig Nelson can be contacted at Craig.M.Nelson@kp.org.

Kathleen Dowling Singh, PhD, a dharma practitioner and transpersonal psychologist, is the author of *The Grace in Dying: How We Are Transformed Spiritually as We Die* and *The Grace in Aging: Awaken as You Grow Older.* Some of the material in her article is adapted from a work in progress, *Spiritual Biography: Viewing Our Lives Through the Lens of Awakening.* To learn more about Kathleen Dowling Singh, visit KathleenDowlingSingh.com.

Robert Sardello, PhD, is co-director with Cheryl Sanders-Sardello of The School of Spiritual Psychology. The School has been in existence since 1992 and offers courses, retreats, and workshops throughout the US and some six other countries. He is also co-editor of Goldenstone Press and the author of seven books, including *Silence: The Mystery of Wholeness* and *Love and the Soul: Creating a Future for Earth.* To learn more about Robert Sardello and The School of Spiritual Psychology, visit www.SpiritualEarthSchool.com.

# INTRODUCTION

*Faith provides evidence for things not seen.*
—Hebrews 11:1

T HIS SOMEWHAT POPULAR quote from the Letter to the Hebrews begins a long and poetic chapter describing the wonders of faith, and how it operates in unique ways from Abel all the way to Jesus. The author describes people of faith as "weak people who were given strength" (11:34) and who thus became "too good for this world" (11:38). Maybe today we would say such people are larger than life—and death—and therefore indestructible.

The entire faith tradition insisted that there was indeed "evidence for things not seen," and yet too often the common notion of faith became something like "whistling in the dark," or a kind of rugged holding-on that equated faith with a dogged perseverance and love of "old time religion"—back when "God was really God." It had little to do with discerning the actual evidence that was commonly available in the present, in the mind, memory, heart, soul, and in creation itself.

Sts. Augustine, Teresa of Ávila, and John of the Cross all found that evidence in the very nature of the soul and its inner workings, but we must admit this was not taught to or experienced by most Sunday Christians. Many formal believers found evidence in Scripture and dogmas that matched and affirmed their personal God encounter, but perhaps even more used Scripture and dogma to make their own experience unnecessary. St. Francis, St. Bonaventure,

Teilhard de Chardin, many poets, and everyday mystics found evidence in the natural world, in elements, seasons, animals, and all living things, but sadly these were often marginalized as mere "nature mystics" or people outside the mainline tradition. Theirs was not "true Transcendence"! This makes one think that we never got our own core message of incarnation, much less its massive implications. This was despite Paul's direct and clear teaching in his Letter to the Romans (1:19–20):

> What can be known about God is perfectly plain since God himself has made it plain. Ever since God created the world, God's everlasting power and deity—however invisible—has been perfectly evident for the mind to see in the things that God has made.

However, like never before in history, this generation has at its disposal a whole new type of evidence, display, and apparition that is proving Paul was correct. And this wonderful evidence is from the discoveries of the scientific mind! Most of us never expected this after centuries of dualistic dismissal of all things rational and scientific. God comes into the world in always-surprising ways so that the sincere seeker will always find, and those on lazy cruise control will find nothing. Is *sincere seeking* perhaps the real meaning of walking in darkness and faith? We must seriously consider this after the very limited good fruit offered by so many "true believers."

The search for truth, the search for authentic love, and the search for God are the same search. I would rather have "one who lays down his life for his friend" (Jn 15:13) by sincere seeking, demanding scholarship, and authentic service, than those who are on no search, do no mental work, and have no open heart for the world, but just want to personally "go to heaven." We have coddled this individualistic *non-Christianity* for far too long, with no encouragement from Jesus whatsoever—"the first goes home at rights with God, and the other does not" being his shocking punch line after setting up a clear contrast between the seemingly sinful tax collector and the religiously observant Pharisee (Lk 18:9–14). The difference is that the tax collector is honest about himself (even though not formally religious) and the Pharisee uses religion to be totally dishonest about himself.

So that you are more likely to read this, and also have time for the other fine articles in this issue, my thoughts on newly appreciated evidence are listed in bullet form.

- The common scientific method relies on hypothesis, experiment, trial, and error. We might call this "practice" or "practices"! Yes, much of science is limited to the materialistic level, but at least the method is more open-ended and sincere than the many religious people *who do no living experiments with faith, hope, and love,* but just hang onto quotes and doctrines. They have no personal practices whereby they can test the faithfulness of divine presence and the power of divine love.

- Most scientists are willing to move forward with some degree of not-knowing; in fact, this is what calls them forward and motivates them. Every new discovery is affirmed while openness to new evidence that would tweak or even change the previous "belief" is maintained. So many religious people insist upon complete "knowing" at the beginning and being certain every step of the way, which actually keeps them more "rational" and controlling than the scientists. This is the dead end of most fundamentalist religion, and why it cannot deal with thorny issues in any creative or compassionate way. Law reigns and discernment is unnecessary.

- The scientific mind has come up with what seem like beliefs; for example, in dark matter, dark holes, chaos theory, fractals (the part replicates the whole), string theory, dark energy, neutrinos (light inside of the entire universe even where it appears to be dark), and atomic theory itself. Scientists teach the realities of things like electromagnetism, radioactivity, field theory, and various organisms such as viruses and bacteria before they can actually "prove" they exist. They know them first by their effects, or the evidence, and then argue backward to their existence.

- Even though the entire world was captivated by the strict cause-and-effect worldview of Newtonian physics for several centuries, such immediately verifiable physics has finally yielded to quantum physics, which is not directly visible to the ordinary observer, but ends up explaining much more—without needing to throw out the other. True transcendence always includes!

- It feels as if the scientists of each age are brilliant, seemingly "right," but also tentative—which creates a practical humility that we often do not see in clergy and "true believers." A great scientist will build on a perpetual "beginner's mind."

- Many scientists believe in the reality of things that are invisible, and thus the active reality of a "spiritual" world, more than do many believers. Thus, although they might be "materialists," they actually have the material world defined with an openness to a "spirit" that they themselves often cannot understand. Is this not "faith"?

Maybe this is all summed up in a quote I jotted down in my journal: "Science can purify religion from error and superstition, and religion can purify science from idolatry and false absolutes. Each can draw the other into a wider world, a world in which both can flourish." And the greatest scientist of our age, Albert Einstein, weighs in with a most succinct conclusion: "Science without religion is lame, and religion without science is blind." So let's walk forward with wide and rich sight!

The very shape, possibility, and meaning of evidence is quickly broadening. Religious people would be wise to get on board. Frankly, I think it is what the Christian desert fathers and mothers, mystics and saints, meant by concrete spiritual "practices," and what the Eastern religions meant by "skillful means." Such "doing it" will give you the kind of evidence that you cannot deny. It will move you into the world of action and beyond the mind to a place where you now "believe" because you know for yourself. Some call it "kinesthetic knowing" or bodily knowing, which is the kind that always wins out in the end anyway.

Richard Rohr, OFM

# Evidential Mysticism and the Future of Earth

*By Michael Dowd*

*We are talking only to ourselves. We are not talking to the rivers. We are not listening to the wind and the climate. Most of the disasters that are happening now are a consequence of that spiritual "autism."*
— Thomas Berry

I AM AN UNABASHED evidential mystic—a sacred realist, a Christian naturalist. Reality is my God and evidence is my scripture. Big History is my creation story and ecology is my theology. Integrity is my salvation and doing whatever I can to foster a just and healthy future for the full community of life is my mission.

Because mysticism entails a profound communion with Ultimacy, great and small, the capacity to experience such communion is unquestionably enhanced by the storied fruit of the scientific quest. The late Catholic "geologian," Thomas Berry, inspired many (myself included) to learn the Universe story, the Earth story, and the patterns of human cultural evolution on a global scale. Together these stories constitute the epic of evolution—what academia now calls the interdisciplinary study of Big History. Thomas encouraged us to go beyond learning the story and to develop our own ways of bringing this Great Story to others. Toward what end? Personal wholeness, of course. But even more important for these times is to cultivate the motivation, the humility, and the breadth of perspective to enable each of us to capably participate in what Thomas called the Great Work of our time.

In this year, the 100TH anniversary of Thomas' birth, I echo his resolve. We desperately need to learn and to tell our shared story of 13.8 billion years of divine creativity. We need to embrace this story, to allow our identities and sense of mission to be shaped by this story, because without it, religion is not nearly enough and the conflict between faith and reason will never end.


## THE EVIDENTIAL REFORMATION

R ELIGION IS UNDERGOING a massive shift in perspective. It is a shift at least as wrenching as the Copernican revolution, which required humanity to bid farewell to an Earth-centered understanding of our place in the cosmos. The religious revolution on the horizon today might well be called the "Evidential Reformation." We humbly shift away from a human-centric, ethnocentric, and shortsighted view of what is important. At the same time, we expand our very identities to encompass the immense journey of life made known by the full range of sciences. In so doing, we all become elders of a sort, instinctively willing to do whatever it takes to pass on a world of health and opportunities no lesser than the one into which we were born.

At the heart of this theological and spiritual transformation is a profound shift in where we find our best guidance regarding two fundamental orientations: *How things are* (that is, *What is real?*) and *Which things matter* (that is, *What is important?*). The shift thus centers on both facts and values—and that means the shift is ultimately about everything.

The good news—the really good news, in my opinion—is that tens of millions of us around the world, secular and religious alike, agree that living in right relationship with reality in the 21st century requires us to value collectively discerned scientific, historic, and cross-cultural insights. The more we move in this direction together, the less our inherited scriptures will continue to divide us.

Religious practices and metaphysical beliefs that arose in particular regions of the world and in response to specific challenges in no way need vanish to make room for a larger and more compelling allegiance. Religions can and do evolve. All we need is to acknowledge that the greatest challenges facing Earthlings today, and the tools to work through those challenges, could not have been fully known by any religious prophet or sage of a bygone era—not Moses, not Jesus, not Muhammad, not Gautama, not Lao Tzu. Worse, we blaspheme the legacies of those leaders by freezing their insights into the pages of written text (a wrong I frame as a form of idolatry: "idolatry of the written word").

This is why an *evidential* worldview has become crucial. We now know that evolutionary and ecological processes are at the root of life and human culture. To disregard, to dishonor, these processes through our own determined ignorance and cultural/religious self-focus is an evil that will bring untold suffering to countless generations of our own kind and all our relations. We must denounce such a legacy. Ours is thus a call to action—a call to sacred activism. Twenty years ago, Carl Sagan both chided and encouraged us in this way:

> How is it that hardly any major religion has looked at science and concluded, "This is better than we thought! The universe is much bigger than our prophets said, grander, more subtle, more elegant. God must be even greater than we dreamed." …A religion, old or new, that stressed the magnificence of the universe as revealed by modern science might be able to draw forth reserves of reverence and awe hardly tapped by the conventional faiths. Sooner or later, such a religion will emerge.[1]

I submit that the "religion" of which Sagan spoke has been emerging for decades, largely unnoticed, at the nexus of science, inspiration, and sustainability. Rather than manifesting as a separate and competing doctrine, it is showing up as a *meta-religious* perspective (again, an insight discerned by Thomas Berry). Such an evidence-based emergent can nourish any secular or religious worldview that has moved past fundamentalist allegiances to the literal word of sacred texts.

A foundation of this meta-religious perspective is the celebration of Big History as humanity's only globally produced, fully inclusive, and evidence-based creation story.


## BIG HISTORY AS THE NEW GENESIS

THE UNIVERSE is a single reality—one long, sweeping spectacular process of interconnected events. The universe is not a place where evolution happens; it is evolution happening. It is not a stage on which dramas unfold; it is the unfolding drama itself. If ever there were a candidate for a universal story, it must be this story of cosmic evolution.... This story shows us in the deepest possible sense that we are all sisters and brothers—fashioned from the same stellar dust, energized by the same star, nourished by the same planet, endowed with the same genetic code, and threatened by the same evils. This story, more than any other, humbles us before the magnitude and complexity of creation. Like no other story it bewilders us with the improbability of our existence, astonishes us with the interdependence of all things, and makes us feel grateful for the lives we have. And not the least of all, it inspires us to express our gratitude to the past by accepting a solemn and collective responsibility for the future.[2]

Big History is the 13.8-billion-year, science-based tale of cosmic genesis—from the formation of galaxies and the origin of life to the development of consciousness and culture, and onward to the emergence of ever-widening circles of care and concern. Through Big History we learn that we are made of stardust and that we're related to everything. Indeed, we can think of our own species as the way the Universe is awakening to the magnificence of its epic journey—a tale of increasing complexity and interdependence. Big History helps us appreciate the role of science in eliciting global wisdom and the role of religion in fostering cooperation at scales larger than our biological instincts could support.

Big History goes by many names. Harvard biologist Edward O. Wilson referred to it as "the epic of evolution." Thomas Berry and Brian Swimme celebrated the evolutionary journey in a 1992 book titled *The Universe Story*. The academic discipline of Big History began in the late 1980s when historian David Christian taught a survey course of this title to college students in Australia. Now, thanks to Bill Gates' enthusiasm (the Big History Project[3]), high school students around the world are learning the story that encompasses all stories and that draws upon all the sciences and humanities.

Big History (by whatever name) is the new Genesis. Ever updated, ever correctable, this universal creation myth—our common creation story—is the source of new facts about our long and storied existence, facts our ancestors could not possibly have discerned. Interpreted meaningfully, Big History promotes a profound sense of kinship and fills us with awe and reverence. We call upon Big History to ignite our zeal to confront the challenges of our times. We easily discern lessons that add zest to the values we already deem vital and vitalizing.

What matters most in how we *use* this new origin story is what has always mattered in the framing and tweaking of a people's sense of inheritance and kinship: how well that story leads us toward *living in right relationship to reality*—that is, in more intimate communion with, and subservience to, God-Nature-Ultimacy.


## EVIDENCE AS MODERN-DAY SCRIPTURE[4]

THE MOST PROFOUND INSIGHT in the history of humankind is that we should seek to live in accord with reality. Indeed, living in harmony with reality may be accepted as a formal definition of wisdom. If we live at odds with reality (foolishly), we will be doomed, but if we live in proper relationship with reality (wisely), we shall be saved. Humans everywhere, and at all times, have had at least a tacit understanding of this fundamental principle.[5]

Increasingly, the generations alive today (the devout included) relate to scientific, historic, and cross-cultural evidence as more authoritative than the dictates of an all-male ecclesiastical body or a literalist reading of Scripture.

An example of this is a 2011 *Christianity Today* cover story, "The Search for the Historical Adam,"[6] which noted that a growing number of evangelical leaders are shedding a traditional reading of Genesis because of what has been revealed through genetic evidence (itself the fruit of science). In the words of Francis Collins and Karl Giberson, "Literalist readings of Genesis imply that God specifically created Adam and Eve, and that all humans are descended from these original parents. Such readings, unfortunately, do not fit the evidence."[7]

Just as Augustine reinterpreted Christianity in light of Plato in the 4TH century, and Aquinas integrated Aristotle in the 13TH, today there are dozens of theologians across the spectrum re-envisioning the Christian faith. Whose ideas are they integrating now? Darwin, Einstein, Hubble, Wilson, and all those who have corrected, and continually contribute to, an evidence-based understanding of biological, cosmic, and cultural evolution.

What we now know (not merely believe) about the challenges of our inherited animal instincts and the vital, creative role of death at all levels of the cosmos is what many find most helpful and also the least disputable.

Without an evolutionary grasp of why our instincts and emotions are the way they are, it isn't just difficult to choose wisely and live our values; it's practically impossible.

WITHIN US ARE instincts shaped by millions of years of evolution. Alas, those compelling drives are now dangerously out of sync with modern times. To be blunt, the very same instincts that enabled our ancestors to survive and reproduce for thousands and millions of years now make many of us fat, some of us addicted, and most of us frivolous in how we use resources and time.

Instincts can hardly be faulted, however. Even many of the poor within our species' wealthiest nations have access to "supernormal stimuli" of a sort and strength that none of our ancestors had to face. Eons of evolution never had to sort through and select against those unhealthy enticements. What are the new and novel allurements that have emerged only in modern times? Certainly processed and abundant foods, feel-good drugs and distilled alcohol, internet porn, romance novels, mind-numbing television, and addictive gaming, along with countless temptations for surrounding ourselves with too much stuff and committing our time to trivial and busy-making pursuits. What this means is that, without an evolutionary grasp of why our instincts and emotions are the way they are, it isn't just difficult to choose wisely and live our values; it's practically impossible.

In 2012 I delivered a TEDx talk in Grand Rapids, Michigan, on the subject of "Why We Struggle and Suffer."[8] I showed, among other things, how evolutionary psychology and brain science give us a far richer appreciation of the mythic wisdom of theological insights such as The Fall and Original Sin. Immediately after my presentation I was approached, independently, by three evangelicals, all of whom said basically the same thing: "Before I heard your talk I was a young earth creationist. Now I've got to accept evolution, I just need to do it in a God-honoring way." One young man, in his mid-20s, put it this way: "I always thought that evolution was about Darwin, DNA, and dinosaurs. I didn't know it was about how to live a more Christ-like life and have healthier relationships."

ALL RELIGIOUS TRADITIONS have offered *beliefs* that helped their adherents face the inevitability of death—and to face it with trust. Thanks to science, we now have *knowledge* that does as much (and more!), while inviting the religious traditions to evolve.

Science not only increases our knowledge, it deepens our intimacy with Reality/God. Nowhere is this more evident than in how an evidential, or sacred-science, worldview helps us honor—indeed, celebrate—the role of death at all scales of the cosmos. As it turns out, everything we value is possible only because of death. The ancients couldn't have known this divine truth revealed by God through science. We can no longer afford to remain ignorant of it; the cost is too high.

Thanks to a dozen different sciences, we can now not only accept, but celebrate, that death is natural and necessary at every level of reality, and death is no less sacred than life.

The following litany expresses "God's evidential word" about the material fact of death at all scales of reality. Science underlies each of the declarations, which I explain in chapter 5 of my book, *Thank God for Evolution*.⁹ If the connections are not obvious to you, consider yourself blessed: wonders await your further inquiry!

*The Gifts of Death*

Without the death of stars, there would be no planets and no life.
Without the death of creatures, there would be no evolution.

Without the death of elders, there would be no room for children.
Without the death of fetal cells, we would all be spheres.

Without the death of neurons, wisdom and creativity would not blossom.
Without the death of cells in woody plants, there would be no trees.

Without the death of forests by Ice Age advance, there would be no
    northern lakes.
Without the death of mountains, there would be no sand or soil.

Without the death of plants and animals, there would be no food.
Without the death of old ways of thinking, there would be no room for
the new.

Without death, there would be no ancestors.
Without death, time would not be precious.

*What, then, are the gifts of death?*

The gifts of death are Mars and Mercury, Saturn and Earth.
The gifts of death are the atoms of stardust within our bodies.

The gifts of death are the splendors of shape and form and color.
The gifts of death are diversity, the immense journey of life.

The gifts of death are woodlands and soils, ponds and lakes.
The gifts of death are food: the sustenance of life.

The gifts of death are seeing, hearing, feeling—deeply feeling.
The gifts of death are wisdom, creativity, and the flow of cultural change.

The gifts of death are the urgency to act, the desire to fully be and become.
The gifts of death are joy and sorrow, laughter and tears.

*The gifts of death are lives that are fully and exuberantly lived, and then
graciously and gratefully given up, for now and forevermore. Amen.*


◆ ◆ ◆


UNTIL WE GRASP that death is no less sacred than life, and
that it plays a vital, necessary role in an evolving cosmos,
Christianity will continue to be shackled by otherworldly
notions of "the Gospel," advanced technologies will prolong physical
and emotional suffering, and the medical industry will inadvertently
underwrite the widening gap between rich and poor.

Few things are more important than transforming how we think
about our inner and outer nature, and our mortality. Thus far, the

Evidential Reformation has been centered in science. Now is the time for our faith traditions to honor evidential revelation—facts as God's native tongue—and carry on the vital tasks of interpretation, integration, and action.

Ours is the prodigal species. Having squandered our inheritance, we are waking up to our painful predicament. Thankfully, God—Reality personified—awaits us with open arms and a welcoming heart. As Thomas Berry would remind us, the entire Earth community is rooting us on! •

# The Perils of Spiritual Faith, Doubt, and Evidence

*By Mark S. Muldoon*

*Faith which does not doubt is dead faith.*
—Miguel de Unamuno

## I

FAITH IS A SLIPPERY TOPIC because it is more about what we don't know, and cannot know in the ordinary sense of knowing, yet we know it to be true to our experience. In the triple theme of the title, the first two have been more traditionally aligned and complementary with one another than the third. If spiritual faith defines itself by what it confronts with doubt, doubt then is part of a seedbed that spawns the growth of faith. However, the dynamic between faith and doubt becomes confounded and maligned when evidence is required.[1] When faith and doubt do not find their completion in rational certainty, the request for evidence undermines and destroys what only faith and doubt alone can achieve—*trust* in a living God.

Spiritual faith is a belief—a belief about meaning in the temporal experience of life. Such a belief involves the believer in an ensemble of historical conceptions, behaviors, and lived experiences that locates meaning in the presence of a transcendental reality—that is, in a reality that does not easily square with the canons of reason and does not exist in the ordinary sense of the word. This reality is the "Other" of our experience. Belief in such a presence will subsist regardless of whether or not evidence supports it, but such subsistence is bought at a price. In a real crisis of faith, the first wish is to find its ground, to rationally justify faith in order to put our full trust in that to which it points.

However, a rationally grounded faith is a contradiction in terms; hence the role of doubt. In the throes of a crisis of spiritual faith, the human reasoning process will clash with the living mixture of physical passion, pride, moral conscience, and the bombast of popular culture. It will become readily apparent that faith is not predetermined but, rather, is seasoned through being questioned by the rigor of human reason. Where human reason will be satisfied with nothing less than guarantees, certainty, and best evidence, a spiritual faith can mature only by constantly struggling against the methodical doubt of reason.

On the other hand—on the other side of crises—faith arises beyond the boundaries of reason as a judgment. A judgment is normally based on sound reasons (evidence) for accepting that a certain claim may be true, but faith is more than a judgment. Pascal's well-worn phrase, "the heart has reasons which reason does not know," reveals that faith indeed has reasons, needs reasons, but goes beyond reasons for believing *that* a transcendental reality exists to actually believing *in* that reality.

This is why faith is often characterized as an "assent" or "leap." It is often realized through subtraction—the subtraction of intellectual dominance over other ways of knowing such as intuition, imagination, and fabulation.[2] This leap or assent is more a choice that involves will, imagination, and love responding to deep-seated desires of our psychic beings. We do not receive revelations like mute favors but are drawn into revelation's discipleship, moving us slowly beyond our fear and doubt to be and to act differently in our everyday world. In this sense, mature faith will always be a response of the whole person, going beyond the known facts of empirical knowledge. Spiritual faith is not straight or linear with our thinking; it is a relationship we have with ourselves, creation, and our belief in creation. Like all relationships, faith can live or die; it bears no temporal guarantees except the historical testimony that many are indeed called to such a relationship.

## II

ONE OF THE CRISES in Christianity today has been the mass exodus from dogmatic faith traditions toward an individualized spirituality. This individualized spirituality defines itself more negatively than positively by simply rejecting the tenets of a dogmatic faith and then looking for some form of personal meaning in the many remnants and shards of religious and philosophical traditions that suit a seeker's needs. Most of this individualized spirituality today is what I would call "deism," which I will speak to later.

In terms of dogmatic faith, various Christian denominations, for example, call upon their faithful to believe in a certain formula encapsulated in a profession of faith such as the Nicene or Apostle's Creed. The former in part: "We believe in one God…God from God, Light from Light…begotten, not made…." Unlike a religio-philosophical position, a revealed religion like Christianity moves away from subjective motivations and spontaneous experiences that would have the faithful believe in a god made of their own individual images and desires. A mature, healthy, dogmatic faith moves the believer away from infantile images and their subjective impact toward a type of listening to revelation over time where the believer wishes to be in contact with God as God, not God as the believer would like the Holy of Holies to be. This movement is toward the Other, the "God from God, Light from Light." Such a movement is actually a rupture in the interior life of the believer, in that God is revealed in unique originality to the believer, that is, not just a reflection of his or her own experiences and needs as being-in-the-world. The lived

# The demand is put on faith to be effective, experiential, and relevant.

experience of Other challenges each of us because such an experience exceeds the limits of our feelings about our own self-worth and the often-mundane reasons we hold for believing we are worthy. This is where the words "call," "gift," and "revealed" become the touchstones of faith in a God not of our own making. Owing to its singularity, dogmatic faith is fraught with doubt and misgivings to the degree it remains individualized and disconnected from historical testimony, tradition, community, and praxis.

In a snapshot, the rise of dogma and doctrine in Christianity is as much about faith as it is about politics. By the second century CE, Christianity had become the dominant religion across much of Europe, Asia Minor, and northern Africa. Yet most believers did not have a firm grasp of what their religion was really about, given over as it was to disparate descriptions of God, the role of Christ, and the basic tenets of faith in a biblical monotheism. Augustine's *City of God* is perhaps the first text to offer a theological understanding of what Christianity envisioned. However, Augustine was a Neoplatonist, and Neoplatonism's dualistic nature had the inherent weakness of being open to indiscriminate mysticism. Anyone could claim a special vision in putting forth God's word. What the budding church needed was a system that laid claim to a more objective authority concerning the meaning of God's word. Hence began the long history of the rise of scholasticism with its underpinning of Aristotelian metaphysics and the forced marriage between revelation and reason. The result, many argued, was that God's word could, ultimately, be known by reason alone, especially by those who understood better than most the proper sequence of inferences that would make them the authorities. A codified body of dogma would come to replace inspiration, intuition, and messy mysticism with certainty. By 1870, this finds its apotheosis in the Vatican I declaration:

If anyone say that the one, true God, our creator and lord, cannot be known with certainty from the things that have been made, by the natural light of reason; let him be anathema.[3]

Since the Enlightenment, we human beings have become more and more situated in a world of our own making, with cyberspace being the emblematic example of the moment. In the last four hundred years, human beings have gained an immense technical and instrumental mastery over nature and realized the historically conditioned nature of knowledge. Such developments have led many to shy away from dogmatic faith, given its embodiment in historical institutions that refused to embrace the ethical demands and compassionate praxis of the dogma being espoused. Consequently, many believe today that, in order to answer the word of God, they should be in a position to discover such truths under their own motivation and know-how. The demand is put on faith to be effective, experiential, and relevant. Dogmatic faith demands as much, but aims at a different end. If I had to summarize—all too quickly—spiritual faith for many today is lived as one form or another of deism.

Deism is a post-Christian position that acknowledges the existence of God, but not the God of revelation. The God of the deist is more of an *idea about God*, described as the highest being, essence, spirit, the infinite, and the good in itself. Such characteristics can be developed in rational proofs so that, eventually, the idea of God comes to belong to the standards of reason. The "God-idea" can be argued for and against on the basis of justified true belief, the epistemological ground from which New Atheism poses its arguments. The result is that such a God-idea really adds nothing to the world. This is a God/god in which I can have faith without submission to religious authority and, since religious authority is not necessary, religious revelation also becomes unnecessary. Further, the idea of God, while acknowledged, has no intervening status in temporal existence since any natural phenomena have a rational explanation, even events that might be claimed to be providential intervention. Moreover, the idea of God lends itself to a type of ecumenicalism, giving it the flavor of being democratic and universal, enabling a type of spiritual melting pot into which all faith traditions might fit. The only container left for such an idea of God is the cosmological one. The personal God of biblical monotheism is eclipsed by a God of awe who is in harmony with cosmic time and space.

In short, deism is a natural theology devoid of any narrative tradition, dogma, and ritual mystery. It sees more in the future than the past. With no need to confront the figure of Christ and the mysteries of a Good Friday theology, the deist is happy to bask in the impressive but lawful complexity of the cosmos and the beauty of nature. God as Other is now tamed to our needs. Like our mastery over nature, God and the spiritual can become instruments to fit our needs for divine companionship, consolation, and trust that something is out there; but it is a trust on our own terms and nicely fitted to our own reasonable categories.

### III

WHEN SPIRITUAL FAITH is reduced to an "idea" that can be fitted into the canons of reason, there is a danger of using faith instrumentally, which in turn kills its spirit. This is true when I demand that my faith be instrumental therapeutically to supply the soothing and consoling I need, to quell my fear of death, to fuel my social-justice agenda, or to justify a type of quietism in the face of moral evil. One contemporary example of faith as an idea which can be reduced to an instrument is the area of addiction research.

There is a great divide in addiction research literature today. On one side are the proponents of "addiction as a brain disease" whose solution is biochemical and therefore warrants more scientific research into neurochemistry. On the other side are those who argue that the reduction of compulsions into a disease like other maladies is unwarranted and contradicted by the legions of recovered addicts of all types who were able to tap into a deeply personal mixture of character, desire, and spirituality.

What divides these two camps is the role of the person. The disease model of addiction as a social policy attempts to separate the human carrier from the biological processes that compose the body and human consciousness. The non-disease proponents contend that, as human beings, we are always more than the sum of our physical parts. Responsibility, choice, human dignity, and spirituality are irreducible aspects of the whole person. Faith sinks into our bodies and minds; it directs us toward unforeseen personal forms of transformation in our thinking and behavior.

Thinking that spirituality might hold a treatment for addicts, psychologists set out to describe spirituality as a motivational trait—that is, a nonspecific, affective force that drives, directs, and tailors our behavior toward a certain end. The hope is to isolate evidence in spiritual practices as an intrinsic source of motivation, making it a stable construct over time that, once accessed, would direct individuals toward particular goals.

Such research is riddled with problems, the most basic being any clarity as to what constitutes spirituality and the parameters that define it. Would such parameters include "transcendence," "meaning/purpose," "wholeness," "consciousness," "relatedness," "creativity," "non-materiality," etc.? Every attempt to define spirituality falls into disarray because the terms associated with the conceptual components of spirituality are highly metaphorical, poetic, and non-literal. They will mean different things to the different people who experience them. As one researcher states in exasperation: "Does any such definition of spirituality offer a valuable contribution to this debate, or is every such definition simply a tautologous rewording of the question of what it means to be human?"[4]

In short, isolating faith as a motivational trait from the totality of the person destroys the very grail for which we search. In wishing to make faith instrumental, the Other of spiritual faith recedes and disappears, since instrumentality banishes the need for trust in a Living God who loves and communicates. Faith used instrumentally

Faith sinks into our bodies and minds;
it directs us toward unforeseen
personal forms of transformation
in our thinking and behavior.

restricts the Other to the confines of the intellect alone; such faith pretends to know what constitutes this love and how it is communicated. This, of course, is idolatry.

In recovery language, it is often said that one cannot be addicted to God *per se*; God as the Other slips from our compulsive need to control and awaits our intellectual assent and surrender.

## IV

WHY IS THERE such a tenacious need to find evidence for the deities we believe in and the faith we have in them? Why will many of us not settle for faith but demand that our gods measure up to our intellectual rigor with proofs and evidence? Why do we curse God and demand an accounting?

In this life, nothing ultimately justifies our worthiness for the existence we have and for the love that we might experience. While conjugal and platonic love will have their part in this, as well as the accolades supplied by popular culture, I believe every living soul desires a completely nonjudgmental, compassionate affirmation of their existence as being "absolutely" worthy of life and love. We want an answer to our cries: "Am I worthy?" "Am I enough, right here and now, on bended knee with my failed dreams, broken hopes, and the ordinariness of my life?" Hence the frenzied search—through love, careers, and a myriad of ventures—for such an affirmation. Tangible evidence of this affirmation, while important, will not be enough to calm the doubt we adults all carry around in our heart of hearts.

What we seek is something the soul already knows. To paraphrase Matthew (3:17), *this is my beloved daughter and son in whom I am well pleased.* Such an affirmation is something for which we can neither beg nor shop. It is freely given but not intended for indiscriminate consumption, yet it is just such an affirmation that, ultimately, human desire seeks. Such an affirmation awaits those who take their doubts seriously while remaining open to the Other. To not have faith in such an affirmation makes a mockery of any honest religious tradition. Faith is a thread that unwinds itself from the fetters of doubt and evidence, pulling us toward the loving arms of the Other—that unique place where our most profound desire finds its true home. •

# Notes on Mystical Evidence

*By James Finley*

I INVITE YOU TO JOIN ME in reflecting on mystical evidence. By that I mean the evidence the mystics tell us we should look for in our efforts to discern whether we are truly on the path that leads to the intimate communion with the God of which the mystics speak with such eloquence.

The practical relevance of mystical evidence becomes apparent when we experience how subtle and delicate the transformative path that leads to mystical union tends to be. We can go for a long time thinking we are not making much progress when, in fact, the union with God that we seek lies waiting to be discovered in a deep acceptance of our poverty and utter dependence on God. And inversely, we can imagine that we are becoming mystics because we are having extraordinary and unusual experiences. Then we realize we have been seduced into clinging to finite experiences that are infinitely less than our true goal of infinite union with the Infinite that reverberates in, even as it utterly transcends, all that feelings can contain and all that thought can comprehend.

When we turn to the mystics for spiritual guidance, we see how they are carrying the torch of mystical awakening that illumines the evidence that lets us know we are on the path that leads to divine union. As we learn to follow the path the mystics mark out for us, we learn to internalize the evidence they have helped us to discover. As we internalize this evidence, we learn to grow in wisdom and inner clarity concerning the deep things of God. In the brief space available to us here, let's reflect on some aspects of mystical evidence.

Before we begin to explore the overtly mystical phases of our spiritual life, the mystics encourage us to look for evidence that we are committed to the lifelong, transformative process of learning to be awake, loving, Christlike human beings.

There is a practical, down-to-earth quality in the writings of the Christian mystics that calls us to be true to the incarnational principle that God is found in the depths of our humanity, in which God in Christ has revealed himself to be present. Here is a passage in the writings of Thomas Merton that bears witness to the importance of grounding our search for God in an honest, vulnerable respect, even reverence, for the gift of our daily lives as human beings. Merton writes:

> Very often, the inertia and repugnance which characterize the so-called "spiritual life" of many Christians could perhaps be cured by a simple respect for the concrete realities of everyday life, for nature, for the body, for one's work, one's friends, one's surroundings, etc. A false supernaturalism which imagines that "the supernatural" is a kind of realm of abstract essences (as Plato imagined) that is totally apart from and opposed to the concrete world of nature offers no real support to a genuine life of meditation and prayer.[1]

The Christian mystics encourage us to look for evidence that we are sincerely seeking to live our day-by-day Christian lives in the down-to-earth, loving manner that Merton describes. They are encouraging us to understand our daily lives of faith in the broad context of the spiritual worldview of contemplative Christianity. According to this worldview, we are to realize that life comes from God and is sustained by God in each passing moment of life on this earth. On this earth we are to

# Mystical experience is God's way of letting us know that we do not have to wait until we are dead to begin to experience the union with the Infinite.

live grounded in this faith, infused with a spirit of Christlike love for ourselves, for others, and for all living things. And we are to live in this way filled with hope, knowing that when death comes our experience of God on this earth, which is mediated through faith, will give way to an unmediated, infinite union with the Infinite that alone puts to rest the restless longings of our minds and hearts.

The essence of mystical experience is not found in visions or in other unusual phenomena that can and sometimes do occur in our lives on this earth. Rather, mystical experience is God's way of letting us know that we do not have to wait until we are dead to begin to experience the union with the Infinite. For even now, on this earth, we can begin to experience mystical states of intimately realized communion in which we and God mutually disappear as dualistically other.

Here, then, is how the mystics are trying to help us. They are helping us to recognize the evidence that lets us know we are being called to more interior, contemplative ways of experiencing God's presence; ways that blossom or come to fulfillment in mystical experience of unmediated, non-dual oneness with God. They are trying to help us recognize the evidence that we are learning from God how to find our way through the obstacles and graces we encounter as we undergo this amazing process of entering into mystical oneness with God.

Each mystic has his or her own way of inviting us to discover the various modes in which we can begin to awaken to more unitive, non-dual ways of experiencing God's presence. They describe the ways this awakening can begin to occur in the hope that, as we read, we will light up inside in recognizing the mystic is describing an intimate oneness with God that we have at least begun to experience. It is this intuitive resonance with what the mystic is saying that provides the evidence we are to look for which helps us to discern and respond to what is happening to us.

The anonymous author of the 14TH-century Christian classic *The Cloud of Unknowing* invites us to discover moments in which we experience the "mysterious action of the spirit in our inmost being stirring us to love."[2]

In the concluding paragraphs of his classic work *New Seeds of Contemplation*, Merton first bears witness to the spiritual worldview of contemplative Christianity by speaking of the mystery of creation in the poetic imagery of a cosmic dance. Merton writes, "The world and time are the dance of the Lord in emptiness. The silence of the spheres is the music of a wedding feast." Then Merton goes on to say:

> We do not have to go very far to catch echoes of that game, and of that dancing. When we are alone on a starlit night; when by chance we see the migrating birds in autumn descending on a grove of junipers to rest and eat; when we see children in a moment when they are really children; when we know love in our own hearts; or when, like the Japanese poet Basho we hear an old frog land in a quiet pond with a solitary splash—at such times the awakening, the turning inside out of all values, the "newness," the emptiness and the purity of vision that make themselves evident, provide a glimpse of the cosmic dance.[3]

We are, at this point, being invited by Merton to ponder those moments in which we experience something of God's presence in such a simple thing as giving ourselves over to the smell of a blood-red rose or lying awake at night listening to the rain. Merton once said in the monastery that there are some things in life that we simply have to accept as true or we go crazy inside. And this is especially so with those moments when we are intimately awakened to a sweet communion with God that we cannot prove to anybody, including ourselves. It is in learning not to break faith in our own awakened hearts that we learn to find the God who is awakening our heart.

God lies in the fact that reason
conquered by love.

The moments in which we are intimately awakened to God's presence in our lives tend to pass away as mysteriously as they came. As they do so, we return to our customary ways of doing things. What the mystics invite us to look for in ourselves is evidence of unconsummated longings that linger on within as each divine visitation dissipates. It is our unconsummated longing for God that inspires, even impels, us to set out on the path in which we learn from God how to live in a more daily, abiding experience of God's presence in each passing moment of life.

The mystics encourage us to look for evidence that we cannot produce by our finite powers alone the experience of contemplative intimacy with God that we are, from time to time, privileged to experience. We can, however, freely choose to assume the inner stance that offers the least resistance to being overtaken by the graced event of oneness with God that we are powerless to attain.

ALL LIFE-CHANGING, TRANSFORMATIVE processes are like this. Lovers are powerless to bring about the moments of oceanic union in which they are renewed and deepened in their love for each other; but they can freely choose to assume that inner stance that offers the least resistance to being overtaken yet one more time by the graced event of experiencing together that oneness in which they renew and deepen their love for each other. Poets are powerless to force the gift of words onto the blank paper; but poets can freely choose to assume the inner stance that offers the least resistance to being overtaken and carried along by the gift of poetry. Those committed to healing are powerless to make it happen; but they can assume the stance that offers the least resistance to the graced event in which healing occurs. So too with us, as we discover the importance of fidelity to some kind of contemplative practice in which we assume the inner stance that offers the least resistance to being overtaken by the graced event of experiencing God's oneness with us in life itself.

Teresa of Ávila invites us to look for evidence that we are being drawn by God into mystical ways of praying that begin with what she calls the prayer of quiet. In the prayer of quiet we are inclined not to say anything to God or to reflect on the things of God. We are, instead, interiorly drawn to sit silently in God's presence. She says, too, that in the prayer of quiet there is often a corresponding tendency to close our eyes. We may also notice a tendency to hold very still, so as not to disrupt the ever-so-subtle sense of God's unseen presence within us and around us as we sit in prayer. Teresa says that, as the prayer of quiet begins to settle in, we begin to realize that the time has come to "think less and love more." She invites us to look for evidence of a newly emerging understanding that our greatest obstacle to finding God lies in the fact that reason has not yet been conquered by love.

Teresa describes the prayer of quiet in such intimate and inviting terms in the hope that we will recognize that we have experienced our own moments of the prayer of quiet she describes. With this recognition comes that inner acknowledgment: "Yes. I have experienced something of the simple attentiveness of which she speaks. The very fact that I recognize and identify with what she is saying names me as someone who has been graced by the delicate moments in which I have yielded to the inner inclination to rest in God resting in me. Or, if I have not experienced the prayer, I can sense in her words that I am being drawn to explore how I might deepen my experience of God's presence by praying in the simple way she describes."

Saint John of the Cross invites us to look for evidence that perhaps we are being led by God into more mystical ways of praying when we experience a dark night in which God gently weans us away from our tendency to overly identify and cling to finite ways of experiencing God's presence. The dark night tends to appear in prayer as the loss of our ability to be nurtured by thinking about the things of God or experiencing his presence in emotional stirrings of inner warmth that let us know God is near. If we do not run away from this powerlessness and aridity in prayer, we begin to notice that we are being led into new, more subtle, non-dual ways of experiencing God's presence. However, we run the risk of not recognizing the ever-so-subtle communion with God that begins to emerge in the dark night if we do not learn to be very patient and attentive to God's unfelt presence. In speaking of sitting in silent prayer, immersed in this dark night, the saint tells us:

Actually, at the beginning of this state the loving knowledge is almost unnoticeable.... But the more habituated he (i.e. the one who prays this way) becomes to this calm, the deeper his experience of the general loving knowledge of God will grow. This knowledge is more enjoyable than all other things, because without the soul's labor it affords peace, rest, savor and delight.[4]

One final and very significant point can be briefly noted; namely, the Christian mystics encourage us to look for evidence that our growing, mystical sense of non-dual oneness with God is drawing us into a heightened sensitivity and response to suffering in ourselves and others. Saint Teresa of Ávila expresses this beautifully in the concluding passages of the seventh mansion that, for her, culminates the mystical experience of God. She say that as we approach this seventh mansion our soul's union with God can be likened to two lit candles with their flames joined as one. When the candles separate, they no longer burn with one flame. She says this is what it is like with us as we rest in mystical communion with God in the optimal conditions of interior peace and silent prayer in which God and our soul rest in oneness. Later, in the stress of the day's demands, we lose our conscious sense of oneness with God until we once again return to the silence and prayer we need to experience oneness with God. She says that once we arrive in the seventh and innermost mansion of the soul, it is no longer like this. For, in arriving at the seventh mansion, our union with God is likened to the rain that falls from the sky into the river, such that we can no longer tell the water that fell from the sky from the water in the river, for the two sources of water have become one. So too, in the non-dual state realized in the seventh mansion, we learn to live in an unbroken, underlying ability to realize that God is as fully present in the messy details of the day's demands as he is in the quiet simplicity of wordless prayer. In this unitive state she says our one concern is, "How can I be helpful?"

We find this same awareness of mystical union with God being inseparably bound up with the real needs of real people—in Merton's insight, toward the end of his life, into the essential bond between contemplation and social justice. And we find this great circularity uniting contemplation and loving service to the world in Richard Rohr's teaching on action and contemplation as well as in the emphasis given to both contemplation and service in the Living School.  •

# Seeing with the Eye of the Heart

By Cynthia Bourgeault

THE WORLD EXISTS in a dynamism, a state of perpetual change and unfolding. Along the whole spectrum of consciousness, from the "endless unity" of the divine Oneness down to the seeming solidity of matter, things are in a state of perpetual motion, a dance of becoming. There is always a kind of cosmic "downloading" going on, as the divine qualities seek new streambeds to flow through; the imaginal realm presses against our physical one in an alchemy of transformation, aching, it seems, to come into finitude. And from our end, we live in the cosmos not as exiles yearning for the absolute but as alchemists and artists, teasing the shape of the divine emerging out of the eternal and into the now.

As the divine reality presses toward form, it tends to do so using images. That's why the realm where it all starts to happen is called the "imaginal." But the imaginal consists of more than just *visual* images: it also includes words and sounds, which share a common root in vibration. "In the beginning was the *Word*," writes the author of the Gospel of Saint John, describing the primordial creative act in its dual and inseparable aspects of purposive intelligence and actual physical vibration.

Because of this dynamism running through the entire gamut of divine manifestation, the Western Wisdom tradition has always suggested that the way we humans get into the dance is through the power of *creative perception*. That is what it really means to *see*, according to Wisdom. Creation itself belongs to the divine. Our role is more a creative midwifery that has to do with intuiting the new patterns as they arise in the imaginal and helping birth them into form.

## THE EYE OF THE HEART

THE INSTRUMENT GIVEN to us to participate in this dance, according to Wisdom, is our *heart*. Not our mind alone, certainly, nor simply the undisciplined riot of our subconscious, but something that both unifies and transcends them from a place of deeper wholeness. Spiritually understood, the heart is an organ of astonishing perceptivity and versatility that when fully awakened and tuned allows us to play our part in the dynamism of creation.

Before we begin our exploration of what this fine-tuning is all about, it is important to touch base with what the heart is *not*, according to the Wisdom tradition. It is not the seat of your personal emotional life. It is not the "opposite" of the head. Rather, it is a sensitive, multispectrum instrument of awareness: a huge realm of mind that includes both mental and affective operations (that is, the ability both to think and to feel) and both conscious and subconscious dimensions. According to the modern Sufi master Kabir Helminski:

> We have subtle subconscious faculties we are not using. In addition to the limited analytic intellect is a vast realm of mind that includes psychic and extrasensory abilities; intuition; wisdom; a sense of unity; aesthetic, qualitative, and creative capacities; and image-forming and symbolic capacities…. They comprise a mind, moreover, in spontaneous connection to the cosmic mind. This total mind we call "heart."[1]

This "spontaneous connection" is an intuitive ability to pick up signals from the imaginal realm. You may have noticed that most of the categories listed have to do with patterns, and that is the heart's genius: it picks up the patterns. That's how it perceives. Beneath the surface of the physical universe, which so often appears "totally random," it discerns the deeper proportion and coherence. This is because it is itself a hologram, a tiny replica of the divine intelligence, and it moves by matching the pattern.

This last point has some very important implications, for it ties the aesthetic and moral realms together. Since the qualities of the divine intelligence begin with love, mercy, and compassion, the heart can only perceive as it comes into alignment with these. It is not possible to "steal" a piece of knowing from the imaginal in order to prop up one's own egoic agendas. Heart-knowing always involves bringing one's whole being into alignment with what is known in an intimate yielding of oneself into the divine intelligence. Creative perception is ultimately, then, an act of love.[2]

## PURIFYING THE HEART

THE BASIC TRAINING in any Wisdom School begins with getting beyond "the fantasies of our own mind"—which for better or worse means bridling the imagination. This is hugely counterintuitive to our own culture, where we prize and even worship the imagination as the source of our personal creativity. But most of what passes for imagination in our modern world, Wisdom would say, is really daydreaming and fantasy. Real imagination—the science of reading the images as they emerge out of the imaginal realm—can begin only after the personal imagination has been brought under control.

For the Desert Fathers and Mothers, and for their successors in both the Benedictine and Orthodox monastic traditions, this work furnished the core curriculum of their respective "schools for the Lord's service." Training in stilling the wanderings of the mind and the emotions was a basic component of monastic discipline, carried out mainly through the rigorous practice of attention in meditation, chanting, and daily work. The goal was to teach the mind to stay put in the present, rather than wandering off into dreams and fantasies.

# Creative perception is ultimately an act of love.

Even when these fantasies seem to be "spiritual," such as visions and messages, the training is still that one has to let them go, for the higher visionary seeing is entered only when the smaller mind has learned not to grab on.

It is an adamant teaching of the Wisdom tradition that the devil (whatever one may take this to be, whether an external or internal contrary force) can only enter a person through the power of the undisciplined imagination. It's when you seize on a fantasy and start to work on it with your emotions and personal agendas that distortion enters. Before it is safe to enter those deeper waters of visionary seeing where the currents of divine passion run hard and deep, the imagination must be contained between the twin banks of attention (teaching it to stay put at a single point) and surrender (letting go of all phenomena as they occur).

## THE SCIENCE OF THE IMAGINATION

So how do you tell the difference between a delusional fantasy and a divine archetype coming into form? Basically, once the heart has mastered the art of staying still, it's the same as with any reading skill: you build comprehension by learning to recognize the patterns.

This brings us to a consideration of one of the greatest Wisdom tools ever developed, which we owe to the Benedictine monasticism of the West. In the Benedictine tradition, the systematic training of the imagination has been carried out primarily through a practice called *lectio divina*, or "sacred reading" of Scripture. To help you visualize the practice, in *lectio divina* a monk works with a short biblical text (no more than a few verses) for an hour or longer in a fluid but disciplined way that involves a rhythmic alternation between each of the poles of three-centered awareness, followed by a plunge into deep stillness.

The practice begins with a slow, out-loud reading of the passage, called *lectio*, allowing it to resonate in the body and engage the moving center. The next stage, called *meditatio*, engages the intellectual center. The monk may visualize, ponder the meaning of the words, or relate the passage to issues in his own life. At some point this intellectual work gives way to *oratio*, or prayer, in which the emotional center begins to resonate. At this point the monk may feel moved to pray or simply to sit with the feelings that the passage has stirred up.

While the exercise of these three centers, individually, is not yet visionary seeing, the next step, which melds them all together, begins to point in that direction. The monk enters *contemplatio*, or contemplation, suspending all mental and emotional activity and simply "resting" in God or in what we might call the transpersonal unconscious. In this state of deep receptivity, the imaginal can begin to stir, melding and quickening the work of all three centers. *Contemplatio* is a bit like weaving the "basket" of the heart around the three "poles" of knowing.

Through gradual, repeated practice at this weaving, the basket grows taller and stronger. Knowledge begins to deepen into understanding, and understanding into visionary seeing. The rich biblical images begin to take on a life of their own. They become the component patterns—a visual "vocabulary," so to speak—by which the monk reads the imaginal.

## THE FOUR SENSES OF SCRIPTURE

ACCORDING TO MONASTIC tradition, this deepening understanding unfolds in four stages. They are milestones on the journey from rational understanding to visionary seeing.

The earliest stage, the literal, is all about facts and linear causality. Does Jesus really intend me to cut off my hand if it leads me into sin? At this level, the Bible tends to be interpreted as a rule book for daily living, and there is little tolerance for ambiguity.

The literal level gradually gives way to something called the "Christological." At this level the monk begins to see all the stories and images in the Bible as pointing directly to the Christ mystery. Jerusalem, for example, is no longer just an earthly city; it is also a symbol of the Church, the "bridegroom of Christ." While this process may seem forced—and if you're not a Christian, even offensive—the *how* of it is actually quite interesting. The monk is leaving linear causality behind and beginning to learn how to see *analogically*, in terms of meaningful coincidences, symbols, and resonance. This is how imaginal seeing actually works, so the training is important.

At the third stage of development, called the "tropological" (which means having to do with growth), the monk leaves behind the Christ mystery as the template and allows the images to form their own patterns and cross-weavings. At this stage the light begins to dawn that the Bible stories themselves are holograms of the soul's journey. They are rich portraits, in analogical language, of the stages and steps we all go through in the process of transformation. Jonah and the whale, for example, is no longer discounted as simply a myth or folktale; we see that every birth into the new involves a fleeing, a sitting in constriction, a darkness, and then a being "coughed up" onto new ground. Once you begin to hear Scripture in this way, it is like suddenly being able to read the imaginal road map.

But there is still a final stage, called the "unitive." At this level of understanding, we become not only sensitive interpreters of the patterns but actual *cocreators*. The fifth-century Desert Father John Cassian once said he knew that his monks had accessed this unitive stage when "they sang the psalms as if they were composing them!" There is an element of primordial, timeless creativity to unitive seeing, as the seeing becomes simultaneously an engendering.

In fact, this is what the word "theology" originally meant. It describes unitive seeing: not talking about God in linear, rational

# The Trinity
# is in fact a mandala
# of the divine dynamism and is
# in that sense one of Christianity's
# most precious treasures.

discourse but actually participating in the *logos* (or creative intelligence) of *theo* (God) as it shapes itself into new forms. The earliest Christian theologians were first and foremost visionaries, and doctrines such as the Trinity did not come into existence through mental calculation but as inspired visions direct from the imaginal world. The Trinity is in fact a mandala of the divine dynamism and is in that sense one of Christianity's most precious treasures. The catch is, however, that only when the unitive stage of understanding is attained can the mandala actually be opened and read.

Indeed, this is one of the most frustrating aspects of being a Christian in our own cultural times. Christianity is a Wisdom path par excellence. It doesn't make sense at the literal level and can actually cause a fair amount of damage. Only when a progressive training of the spiritual imagination opens up the unitive capacity in a person does Christianity become congruent with its own deepest truth.

When the heart is pure, it sees straight into the imaginal world. And here is where the joy of the dance really begins. People who have honed their heart are trustworthy to move between the realms and take their places as artisans and midwives of the divine becoming. They become "theologians" in the true sense of the word, helping to bring into existence the new forms and insights through which humanity continues to receive its daily bread.

It's marvelous to see how this sacred creativity works. I think of the small monastic community at Taizé, in France, where Brother Jacques Berthier began out of "thin air" to create a new form of Christian sacred chanting, which has spread like wildfire around the world, capturing people (particularly young people) by drawing them once again into the depth of the Mystery.

## THE GIFT OF CONSCIENCE

THERE IS A SUBTLER and more personal artistry that goes on once the eye of the heart is opened. Conscience is another of those terms whose meaning in the language of Wisdom is very different from our usual cultural reference points. It is not the conditioned voice of your moral upbringing. Rather, *it is the heart's own ability to see the divine hologram in any situation, no matter how obscured, and to move spontaneously and without regard for its personal well-being in alignment with that divine wholeness.* When conscience awakens in a person, it brings not only the obligation but also a mysterious ability to be present in exactly the right way.

Say, for instance, as in that fabled story told of Saint Francis of Assisi, you would spontaneously embrace the leper standing before you because the eye of your heart would tell you that only *that* gesture would restore the image of God in the brokenness of the situation. Or like Jesus, you would accept death on a cross rather than meeting violence with violence.

Conscience is the pearl of great price; it is both the instrument and the supreme realization of visionary seeing. It is the capacity always and everywhere to see the whole of God yearning to become manifest in all our human beings and doings, like the full of the moon faintly present behind the crescent. With the awakening of this eye, you no longer see Wisdom; you *are* Wisdom. •

*This article is excerpted from Chapter VII, "Seeing with the Eye of the Heart," of Cynthia Bourgeault's* The Wisdom Way of Knowing *(San Francisco: Jossey-Bass, 2003). This material is reproduced with permission of John Wiley & Sons, Inc.*

# Transcendent Faith, Transcendent Art in the Rothko Chapel

*By Susan J. Barnes*

*Through art, God constantly clears the path to our heart.*
—Dominique de Menil

O N APRIL 17, 1964, John and Dominique de Menil visited the New York art studio of Abstract Expressionist Mark Rothko. They invited him to make a cycle of paintings to decorate a chapel in their adopted home of Houston, and he accepted. The chapel was intended for the Roman Catholic University of St. Thomas, a young liberal-arts college whose campus and academic programs the French-born couple had been helping to develop. It was to be the capstone of the master-planned mall.

Instead, the modern art monument now known as the Rothko Chapel was dedicated on February 27, 1971, as the world's first broadly ecumenical center, an independent entity "welcoming all faiths and belonging to none." Among other things, it quickly became a pioneering institution honoring human rights and a distinguished, visionary center hosting inter-religious dialogue, including international colloquia, as well as a place where individuals come to meditate and congregations of many different faiths are welcomed to worship.

A transformative expansion of the chapel's mission, ministry, and audience had occurred in the seven years between its commission and the dedication. That itself is evidence of things unseen. How it happened is the story I want to tell, and it began long before the commission itself.

If you think about the art adorning any Catholic church—medieval to modern—you might find it curious that someone would give such a commission to an abstract artist of Jewish origin, but it never occurred to John and Dominique de Menil to ask anyone else. It never occurred to them *not* to give Rothko free reign in his creation. Nor did it occur to Rothko to turn them down.

In 1964, Rothko was 61 years old, John 60, and Dominique 56. They had the wisdom of their years, the vision of what they might accomplish, and the energy to undertake it.

Though all three were émigrés, the painter's background and life experiences were quite different from his patrons'. The Russian-born Rothko was certainly known and admired, but had just begun to know financial success. John de Menil was CEO of Schlumberger, Ltd., the oil-exploration services company founded by his father-in-law, whose operations he had brought to the Americas after the fall of France in World War II. Social and civic activists in Houston, he and Dominique had been collecting art seriously for twenty years and supporting museums there as well as in New York and Paris.

Dominique and John were Catholics; she was devout. Rothko had been an ardently religious Jew as a child, but had no religious practice as an adult.

The three of them shared an unspoken faith, however, which brought them to the commission. It was not about denominational religion. Instead it was faith in something else "unseen," in the power of great art to transcend every kind of limitation, including language, doctrine, even thought, and to speak directly to the spirit—the kind of art that was right for a chapel. The Menils knew Rothko created that type of art.

Rothko aspired to nothing less. As early as 1943 he wrote, "only that subject matter is valid which is timeless and tragic." His mature paintings are large and consist of one or two colored rectangles floating on a background of another color. Devoid of any images or symbols, they invite (even challenge) the viewer to a direct encounter with the presence of the work of art. Although Rothko realized that many people would not understand, he took the risk for those who would because, as he wrote, "A picture lives by companionship, expanding and quickening in the eyes of the sensitive observer." In one-man shows and in work on a previous (undelivered) multi-painting commission for the Four Seasons Restaurant in New York City, he learned that his work was most effective as an environment.

The chapel commission was the artist's dream come true. And though Rothko did not live to see the paintings installed in Houston, when he had completed them he wrote to the Menils:

> The magnitude, on every level of experience and meaning, of the task in which you have involved me, exceeds all my preconceptions. And it is teaching me to extend myself beyond what I thought was possible for me. For this I thank you.

BOTH AS AN ENSEMBLE of paintings and as a center for contemplation, dialogue, and social justice, the chapel's destiny would far exceed all of the Menils' expectations as well. But neither John nor Dominique de Menil was surprised that the Rothko Chapel transcended their vision. After all, it had begun, in Dominique's words, as "an act of faith." From the outset, the chapel belonged to God.

God was clearing a path for the Rothko Chapel that had been laid long before in the hearts and lives of the patrons by their love for one another. Although her father, Conrad, was an avowed atheist, Dominique Schlumberger had been reared in the Protestant tradition of her family. From childhood she'd had a deep spiritual longing, and her conversion to Catholicism after her marriage was a profoundly personal spiritual matter. Like the vast majority of his countrymen, John de Menil was Roman Catholic. French Catholic enmity toward Protestants, dating back five hundred years to the Reformation, was on the rise again in the 1920s when the couple met. Marriage to a Protestant was not sanctioned by Catholicism. Their union could not and did not receive the Church's blessing.

Though their love transcended those cultural divisions and prejudices, the couple did not dodge or dismiss the issue. Instead, with characteristic intelligence, clarity, and integrity, they faced it together. According to William Middleton, who is preparing the biography of the Menils, "Many of their earliest exchanges involved passionate discussions of religion." William graciously shared the following examples from their premarital correspondence. Dominique wrote:

> We are brought together by the most human emotion—love—and by our common belief in God. As long as we are united in this feeling and in this belief, neither churches nor rules nor pastors nor priests will be able to keep us apart.

John wrote:

> For those of us who are Christians, it comes down to a very few simple elements. I believe in God, our Father who art in Heaven. Everything is contained in those few words. All the rest is just custom, dogma, of little import.

Their own experience and their natural open-mindedness made the Menils sympathetic to the nascent ecumenical movement in the 1930s. More stones were being laid on the path toward the Rothko Chapel when Dominique attended talks on ecumenism by the Dominican, Fr. Yves Congar, in 1936; they "marked me for life," she recalled. Describing in retrospect the role those talks had played, Dominique used the Gospel metaphor of the mustard seed (Mt 13:31–32): the tiny seed from which an enormous plant would grow. Another of Jesus' metaphors from the Gospel of Matthew fits, too: Congar's ecumenical vision was a seed sown on ground so fertile that it would yield more than a hundredfold.

At that stage of their lives, the Menils had not yet discovered their passion for art and collecting. That, too, would be nurtured by a French priest after their move to the United States. The couple first met Fr. Marie-Alain Couturier in liberal Catholic circles in Paris. As it happened, Fr. Couturier was on the US side of the Atlantic when France fell in 1939. Thus he spent the war years in New York, where a number of modern French painters—including Surrealists—had also fled. When the Menils visited Couturier in the city during 1943–45,

# "We are brought together by the most human emotion—love—and by our common belief in God."

they visited galleries with him and met a number of artists. They bought the first works in a collection that would grow to number in the thousands. Today it is known as The Menil Collection in Houston, a museum which opened in June 1987 down the street from the Rothko Chapel.

Fr. Couturier returned to France as a champion of modern art and an advocate for a renaissance of the Church as patron. He sought "to bring to an end…the absurd divorce which for the past century has separated the Church from living art…[and] to appeal to the greatest of independent artists, no matter what might be their personal convictions."

Putting words into action, Fr. Couturier played a role in four major church commissions: Le Corbusier's church at Ronchamp, Matisse's Chapel of the Rosary at Vence, Léger's mosaic facade for a church in Assy (which also contains works by Bonnard, Braque, Chagall, Lipchitz, Matisse, and others), and Léger's stained glass windows for Sacré-Coeur, Audincourt.

The Menils saw these projects on visits to France. Fr. Couturier remained a close friend and an influential one. Their later choice of the lapsed-Jewish artist Rothko to make the decorations for a Catholic chapel was perfectly in line with Couturier's own philosophy and projects.

Although Rothko and the Menils had not yet met, their paths began to merge in their common attraction to Surrealist painting. Mark Rothko and other New York artists of his generation were powerfully influenced by Surrealist art, imagery, and ideas, particularly in the 1940s, after encounters with the expatriate artists themselves.

Among the characteristics of Surrealism are a taste for the unconscious, the non-rational, the archetypal, the primal, the inexplicable,

"This chapel...is rooted in the growing hope that communities who worship God should find in their common aspiration the possibility of dialogue with one another in a spirit of respect and love."

and the mysterious. Some Surrealist paintings depict recognizable images, objects, or forms in confounding combinations or juxtapositions. Others have abstract imagery. Many are dreamlike, as Rothko's were through the 1940s. Though his mature style is utterly devoid of images, it is nonetheless charged with meaning, as was his earlier work.

The Menils avidly collected Surrealist paintings from the 1950s and later—particularly works of Max Ernst and René Magritte. Surrealist taste also underlay other kinds of art strongly represented in their collection: tribal—particularly African—art and pre-classical ancient art, including Paleolithic objects and Bronze Age pieces from Asia Minor as well as outstanding Cycladic figures. These works from disparate cultures have in common both esthetic beauty and innate power. One sensitive critic told me, after visiting the newly opened Menil Collection, "I get it. It's all about the Spirit." Today she might say "oneing."

Having lived with several of Rothko's paintings before the chapel commission, the Menils knew that they, too, had a similar transcendent beauty and power.

For some time, Rothko had preferred to have his paintings installed with one another rather than with those of other artists. The chapel commission gave him a long-sought chance to make a series of paintings which were conceived as a whole for a space created specifically for them. He chose an octagonal floor plan, whose walls surround the viewer within the painted environment. The central-plan space invites the viewer to be still; so, too, does the contemplative palette of his great murals: dark maroon and black. Both proved hospitable not only to meditation and worship, but also to musical and literary events as well as gatherings in which widely diverse experiences and opinions were shared in respectful dialogue.

Rothko finished his paintings for the chapel in 1967 and put them into storage pending the construction of the building. Before it could be built, the Basilian Fathers of St. Thomas wisely realized that it would be an artistic monument of importance in its own right and not practical as a university chapel. The Menils understood the Basilians' decision not to accept the gift. Spurred by the revolutionary ecumenical vision of the Second Vatican Council, their own sense of the chapel's possibilities was beginning to take flight. They built the chapel on land they owned just west of the St. Thomas campus, where it could and did serve the university until its own chapel was built years later.

The Menils had purchased a cast of Barnett Newman's *Broken Obelisk* in memory of Dr. Martin Luther King, Jr. Shortly after construction began on the Rothko Chapel, the Menils made the decision with Barnett Newman to place the sculpture in a reflecting pool on axis with the entrance. Prominently placed and lit through the night, the simple, elegant conjunction of the two ancient forms—an obelisk inverted atop a pyramid—stands as a bold beacon of their commitment to human rights.

The Rothko Chapel's dedication was celebrated with Jewish, Muslim, Orthodox, Catholic, and Protestant clergy in attendance, as well as representatives from the Vatican and the World Council of Churches. Dominique de Menil captured the spirit of that great occasion—the spirit that would direct the chapel's multi-faceted future:

> This chapel is rooted in the growing awareness that love and the search for truth are unifying principles. It is rooted in the growing hope that communities who worship God should find in their common aspiration the possibility of dialogue with one another in a spirit of respect and love.[1]

In her brief, eloquent address she also remarked on "the providential thread" running through the events that had brought them to that day. The energy of the unseen had carried painter and patrons to create something that none could have imagined only a few years before. Originally conceived to serve a small, Catholic university, the Rothko Chapel had been born free of any sectarian ties, enabling it to serve the whole of God's people.

Evidence, indeed.

*This reflection is based on two studies of my own: the monograph history,* The Rothko Chapel: An Act of Faith, *and a talk I gave on February 19, 2011, at the chapel, in their 40th anniversary series. I am grateful to Barb Nicol; to Emilee Dawn Whitehurst, Executive Director, and Suna Umari, Archivist, of the Rothko Chapel; and to William Middleton, a tiny portion of whose research is cited here. In addition to Middleton's eagerly awaited biography of the Menils, I highly recommend the volume of collected writings by Dominique de Menil,* The Rothko Chapel: Writings on Art and the Threshold of the Divine, *as well as* Art and Activism: Projects of John and Dominique de Menil, *Josef Helfenstein and Laureen Schipsi, ed.*

.

# Curing and Healing

*By Craig M. Nelson*

MY LIFE WORK has allowed me to merge multiple paths: as a tenured clinical scientist from a medical laboratory; as a lecturer on early Christian thought, religion, science, creation, and evolution at a local state university; and as a clinical ethicist. The intent of this essay is to highlight how these paths have led me to understand the convergence of curing and healing.[1] This convergence does not take place in the laboratory, the lecture hall, or at the bedside. It happens within people through synthesis and sojourn.

Monica Hellwig[2] reminds us that there is no profane sphere and that what grounds religious contemplation is the action of remaining humble before the Holy, and open to the word of God and all that God is doing: the present and unique experience in one's personal life, often shaped and influenced by a religious tradition. My personal action and contemplation has been as a sojourner in a grace-filled world. In the marketplace my challenge has been to look for and connect with the "hidden Holy" permeating the busyness of everyday life.[3]

# Curing is what medicine attempts.

In my clinical ethics practice I find complementarity between curing and healing. In my professional experience, curing is primarily viewed through the lens of clinical science and the understanding of disease processes, while healing often expands curing to include the emphasis on a moral commitment to human dignity and its demands, shaped by a theological lens.

One goal of honoring human dignity is to help discover a unity between the patient as a person, scientifically examined, and as a subject of moral justice. The good of the patient is sought, in their particular existential circumstance,[4] through both curing and healing. In the medical encounter, the good of the patient has texture and complexity when observed from the patient's point of view. Restoration, worthwhile life, and coping with brokenness at different moments in life highlight the dignity of the patient's horizon.

Curing is what medicine attempts. Healing is what all of us do together. I make this distinction because, in my frequent encounters with health care providers, patients, and families, sometimes healing and curing become conflated. They are related but different.

In curing, the biomedical paradigm stresses that we can account for disease by examining the deviation of measurable biological variables from the norm. We use the language of chemistry and physics to explain biological systems and their phenomena. Disease is often conceptualized in terms of the disordering of underlying physical mechanisms. Somatic parameters are monitored and, once they fall back into the norm, people are cured. From septicemia to heart health, curing can and does happen. When curing happens, we are grateful.

Yes, healing can involve curing, but curing does not exhaust healing. Healing is more existential. In healing we give each other that human something—a word, a look, a gesture, authentic presence. Imparting human caring and kindness is often far more compassionate than imparting theories and techniques. When I encounter colleagues and patients, we may never precisely quantify what we give each other in the encounter, but somehow we walk away changed for good. This is what makes the healing journey meaningful. It is this "I/Thou"[5] interaction that makes it tolerable to be with the dying and to cry for human loss. We have done something wonderful, even if we aren't sure how to name what we have done. By being with our patients and families on their journeys, by showing them our concern and using our professional training, we inspire them to find a "why" to living and discover one for ourselves too. The important question in making sense out of human suffering becomes: "How can we discover anything meaningful in it?"

To illustrate what I mean, I offer three examples of "existential" healing. Years ago, as a young medical ethicist, I was asked to be part of a Lenten panel for elders at a local parish. They were reviewing their lived values and treatment preferences as they began to prepare their advance directives for health care. They showed great interest in the other speakers present: a palliative care physician, a social worker, and a nurse. I was the youngest person in the room. I tried to connect with the audience when I spoke but I did not succeed. In fact, I bombed. The evening could not end soon enough and I learned from this experience that I had a long way to go to become an effective, seasoned ethicist. As is usually the case after a speaking session, people began lining up near the speakers to ask more questions or tell them how much they liked their presentation. No one was making their way to me and I was eager to begin the "walk of shame" out of the parish hall. I hurriedly stuffed my presentation material into my briefcase, heading for the door.

As I began to leave, a frail lady approached me and asked if I was the one who said he was an ethicist. I said yes and she asked me if I had a minute. It so happened that her husband had recently had treatment withdrawn while he was in the process of dying. She felt she had not served her husband or church the way she should have. She was the only one who approached me. In fact, we were the last ones to leave. That evening I discovered a healing approach to ethics practice, using my clinical knowledge as a "listener" as I helped a loving wife who had recently said goodbye to her husband of many years. Narrative ethics, the moral guidance of the Church, and the clinical insight of a scientist converged. "Tonight will be the first night in months

# Healing is what all of us do together.

that I will go to bed with a peaceful heart," she said. This sweet little frail woman was why I was invited to be part of the Lenten panel.

How does this encounter exemplify existential healing? In describing the clinical experience of her husband, she also voiced the *sapientia cordis* of her experience. This is understood as pre-reflective ontological understanding or, more simply, wisdom of the heart. All people have some of this. I have been trained to listen for it in personal narrative, to draw it out, and to help it stand tall. This involves recognizing innate moral inclinations and being a source of exhortation for them. The encouragement of the listener is effective when it leads the person telling their story to become "good" from their own wisdom of the heart and strive to act out their own moral goodness. They become moved to do good by the affective nature of inner moral sense, informed by an inner moral compass. This woman knew that biological life was precious and should be respected. She also valued her inner belief in continuing life with God beyond the physical realm. Together we connected the two from her perspective of faith and love.

V IKTOR FRANKL[6] reminds us that we form "footprints in the sand of time." Nothing can be undone or done away with. Jean Vanier[7] echoes this same understanding when he emphasizes that we are not going to achieve great things, or be heroes, but simply live each day with new hope, like children, in wonderment as the sun rises and in thanksgiving as the sun sets. Existential healers can plant the seeds of eternity, visible in small and daily gestures of love, forgiveness, and presence. I somehow have been changed "for good" by others, and so have they. Joy and richness have been exchanged along with suffering and sadness.

My next example of existential healing is from the hospital setting, where a Catholic family was struggling with conscience. Late on a Friday afternoon, my pager went off. I was summoned to a family meeting to assist a wife struggling to both follow her husband's wishes and honor the understanding she had of her faith. A social worker and a physician from the ICU were waiting for me to meet with this woman and her family. Her husband had sustained a severe brain injury from lack of oxygen and was developing extreme multi-organ failure. His kidneys were shutting down and blood pressure and heart rate were very unstable. Her husband had clearly stated

# Existential healers can plant the seeds of eternity, visible in small and daily gestures of love, forgiveness, and presence.

that if he were in this condition he would not want to have his dying prolonged and would want to let nature take its course. His wife believed that if she gave permission to treat his symptoms, keep him comfortable, and forego dialysis and maximum vasopressor treatment for his instability—in other words, let nature take its course—she would be violating church teaching and could not receive the sacraments. Her pastor had not given her supportive guidance and she was very tearful. I listened to her faith narrative at length and reflected back to her what I heard her say. We talked about how she was describing the largeness of God and the absolute good of valuing a relationship with God, even valuing it more than biological life. I asked her: "Are there limits to preserving biological life?" "What are the ways God calls people home?" The more we talked, the more she seemed filled with solace. She finally looked at me and said that she felt more at ease about her husband's path of letting go and felt she could now approach the sacraments with a peaceful heart. As she thanked me, I thanked her for sharing her inner heart with me.

Existential healing was again evident. The science of medicine could offer no lasting hope for this dying man. The family's deep wisdom of faith needed acknowledgment. Together they formed a healing synergy. All that could be done had been done and it was time to let the peace of faith flow.

My final example is from our current clinic for patients with amyotrophic lateral sclerosis (ALS), also known as Lou Gehrig's disease. A team of health care professionals meets with patients and their families once a month. The team includes a neurologist, a pulmonologist, a registered nurse, a physical therapist, an occupational therapist, a respiratory therapist, a registered dietitian, a chaplain, an ethicist, support professionals from the local ALS Association, and often consultants for state-of-the-art support technology. Our service provides a one-visit clinic so patients can meet with multiple health care providers each time they have an appointment. My role as ethicist involves decision-making assistance and addressing moral distress for patients, family members, and the health care team.

The clinic began seeing patients in 2012. The clinical course for ALS can be varied. We were all aware that we would accompany our patients through every phase of their journeys. By the time patients began to enter their final days, relationships had grown deep and reciprocal. Because we grew to know our patients very well, saying goodbye was a steep emotional mountain to climb. Moral distress hovered over the treatment team. We participated in a reflective exercise that would help us begin to process death and dying from our own sacred ground. We began to concretely sense that meaning is experientially discovered, not defined or given. Our time of reflection emphasized valuing a "why" to live, wisdom of the heart, the beauty of Jean Vanier's simplicity, and some therapeutic music about being changed for "good" from both a patient and health provider perspective.

As we embraced existential healing we discovered that the "epistemic" knowing, which emphasized the clinical understanding of medical limits and possibilities, was more of a process than an epiphany. Patients are always eager for the newest medical breakthroughs to help them concretize life goals. Patients try to breathe in the wisdom of how to *live* their lives in spite of their looming finitude. This was the gift of *phronesis,* or wisdom. They could discover their *why* in facing their *how.*

Healing is a place with open spaces. While we never stop valuing "things measurable" as medicine cures, healing can quench our deepest thirst. Our encounters in the everyday world are where the two intertwine and provide unique opportunities for curing and healing to comingle.  •

# Full Circle:

## The Evidence of Love

By Kathleen Dowling Singh

*The eye through which I see God*
*is the same eye through which God sees me;*
*my eye and God's eye are one eye,*
*one seeing,*
*one knowing,*
*one love.*
—Meister Eckhart

THOMAS KEATING REMINDS US that we are all on a spiritual path simply by the good fortune of our human birth. Here we are, on this beautiful planet with our precious human lives. We live these fleeting lives as an expression of love. We live formed of love and, at every moment, suspended in love. Our origin, the very ground of our being, is love. And love, as Thomas Merton realized, is our true destiny.

Love, the sacred formless, continuously gives rise to forms. Yet for so many of us, for so much of our lives—as much as we might long for the Sacred or actively search for it—we don't *know* love, that welcoming holy essence of our own being. For the most part, we don't feel it, we don't embody it. We don't pause endlessly and gratefully in awe of love.

We pass our lives, instead, almost by default, in the congested, often confused, energy of our sensations and conceptions, in the defended energy of a separate sense of self. We spend much of our lives ignorant of the love in which we live and move and have our being. We see love, the very presence of the Sacred, as an attainment for which we've strived or hoped. We see love as something that we do not, at the moment, know to be real and true. We do not, in our ordinary, everyday minds, recognize love as our ever-present ground, our hallowed Reality.

Ordinarily, we operate only within our egoic self and the tense universe that self creates. Knowing only form, there is no evidence to be found for the sacred formless that we've intuited and for which we have longed since we were children. It is unknowable to, unreachable by, our untransformed senses and the assumptions of our thoughts. We may have had a few interludes where thinking ceased temporarily and the heart was allowed to know what it knows. We may be fortunate enough to hear spiritual teachings, words that concern more than self, more than form only, and we resonate with them, however fleetingly at first.

The resonances arise as tiny, clear notes within our confusion. Without knowing for ourselves the presence of the Ground of Being, the *Dharmakaya* as Buddhist practitioners refer to it, without abiding in it, the small, clear callings of love and truth are quickly forgotten or merely frustrate us with their seeming elusiveness.

Some of us strive with great effort for a "spiritual experience," while others get trapped in the discouragement of believed unworthiness. Some of us end up posturing goodness and piety, tightening our grasp on dogma and philosophy. Some of us cross our fingers and hope that the words we hear are true. We may end up with the hope that believing the words enough will magically make them so, not yet realizing that the truth is only transformative when we know it as such for ourselves.

I N ALL OF OUR different ways we engage in the great search for love, the search for the ground of our own being—as if it were elsewhere. Our love of God, of truth, of mystery, leads our longing. Love fuels our search and we respond to its call as it seeps through the cracks in our loveless armor. Our seeking is driven by love, although we sadly proceed within the great confusion of thinking that love is a concept we can learn. We fall prey to the inflexibility of beliefs and block our experience of the divine presence with our own mental images of the Sacred. We become seekers who put great effort into believing and place great value on the self who is seeking.

Over time, we discover that great effort only sustains the sense of self, the very obstacle to love. And, if we are committed enough in our longing to respond to love's call, we come gradually to see that beliefs are not evidence. They produce a feigned faith, an ego's act of will. Beliefs will get us nowhere on the spiritual path. Beliefs have no currency, nor are they current. They have nothing to do with the present's disclosure of the Sacred.

No belief, no conceptual thought—the home of most of our secondhand experience for most of our lives—can ever meet the Sacred. Conceptual thought removes us by degrees of elaboration from this very moment, the only moment where love is ever, always, and already disclosed—offering, welcoming, grounding, gracing.

T HIS GIFT of a precious human life came *sans* operating instructions. Although every breath we take is love captured in form, as Sufi mystic Llewellyn Vaughan-Lee so beautifully put it in a personal correspondence with the author, we're lost and confused, and looking for love in all the wrong places.

St. Bonaventure recognized that within this precious gift of a human life are enfolded three tools for knowing the three domains that are available to our life-in-form. Each of us possesses the eye of the senses for perceptual knowing, the eye of the mind for conceptual knowing, and the eye of contemplation for the knowing—the direct realization—of the Sacred, far beyond the senses and the intellect.

We have, of necessity, made use of and placed great reliance upon our physical senses and our intelligence. They have allowed us to survive as a species. We have developed well-honed capacities for adaptation and survival, keeping our eye out for the wooly mammoth around the bend, scheming about how to grow the most grain on the

# Love fuels our search and we respond to its call as it seeps through the cracks in our loveless armor.

plot we've ingeniously cleared, and checking out how much the guy on the other side of the trees is managing to grow.

We continue, tens of thousands of years later, to rely almost exclusively upon the eyes of the senses and the intellect. We are far beyond the point where it serves our individual and species' purpose to continue to live not knowing love, not knowing the Sacred. Doing so, we persist in living a life of only self, only form, allowing fear and desire to lead us as if they knew what they were doing.

Relying upon only our senses and conceptual mind, we have created an experience of existence marked by separation: separation from others, from our own essential nature, and from the Sacred. We have passively allowed the unexamined mind to fabricate narrow horizons, imaginary boundaries that keep us from knowing the vast, astonishing light of our own being.

THE EYE of the senses functions to discern the physical forms of the world, keeping us from tripping over our shoelaces. The eye of the intellect can hold and discern mental formations, the conditioned meaning we bestow upon appearances. Ordinarily, neither sees clearly. Our typically unexamined perceptions and conceptions are conditioned by the sense of self, obscuring the truth of what is so in any moment.

The eye of the senses, for example, can only see light wave refractions and yet we, never deeply investigating the dynamics, believe that we can directly see desks, garbage, or sunsets. The ears can only detect vibrations through the atmosphere, and yet we, again never deeply investigating the dynamics, imagine that we can directly hear a mourning dove, an alarm clock, or the Rolling Stones. We take a lot for granted.

The moment that we begin to deeply investigate, as Werner Heisenberg did for example when he explored the principle of uncertainty, we see that the eye of the senses betrays us into believing in a world of fixed and separate entities, of nouns, just as we conceive of them and therefore perceive them. The observer is involved in every perception, overlaying conditioned memory upon a never-before-arisen present. It serves us to make these shortcuts in our everyday life, to be sure, but we deepen our basic confusion when we take those shortcuts for granted. When we take our own mental images as truth without investigation, we miss the dazzling display of life loving itself.

In the same way, the eye of the intellect, the eye of conceptual mind, constructs the world according to its own conditioned beliefs. We see what we want to see in accordance with whatever paradigm with which we've become familiar, with which we identify, and which we unreservedly believe to be true. Witness the horrifying polarization in our country at the moment. Facts that do not fit the cherished paradigm to which the egoic self so tightly clings are resisted, denied, and twisted. Ignorance—the willingness to ignore what's so—reigns supreme when the eye of the mind operates in stubborn confusion, without clarity.

WE MAY SPEND a long time looking for love with eyes that cannot see it. We spend so much of our lives searching for that which propels us, that in which we already abide and are sustained. Fueled by love's longing, we look for that which is looking.

When we look for the Sacred with the untransformed eye of the senses, we may hope for and cling to visions, experiences, or moments of deep feeling or emotionality. Doing so, we reaffirm the experiencer, the feeler, the visionary, the seeker—the very separate self-sense that obscures love.

When we look for the Sacred with the eye of the intellect, our mental images of the Sacred and all of our beliefs about it are themselves the obstacles to the divine presence of formless awareness. We may get caught in doctrine and philosophy, the information of transformation. Doing so, we will only posture our spirituality, giving sterile lip service to the Sacred. We will bear no fruit.

THE SAINTS AND SAGES from every wisdom tradition have recognized that "unless thine eye be single" (Mt 6:22), we cannot touch the truth. It is only through the eye of contemplation that we can realize and come to know our essential nature and the essential, holy nature of all things. When we are lost in conceptuality's noisiness, the Sacred is obscured. It is the contemplative eye that gives rise to the stillness necessary to see, to rest in grace, to abide in love.

Stillness is not about the cessation of thought, necessarily, but about resting in the still awareness in which thought is occurring. Contemplative practice allows awareness to remain silent and unwavering, like a candle in a windowless room. Such stillness disembeds us from ego and conceptual mind. Using the contemplative eye, we discern the stunning revelation of the Sacred.

The eye of spirit, once engaged, no longer so easily turns over its precious realization to conceptualizing, like ransom to a usurper king. We have let the conceptual mind hold us hostage for too long and have suffered in confused searching as a consequence. Beginning to live within the contemplative eye, having tasted Reality, we are no longer willing to settle for the thin gruel of concept.

With that revelation of Presence, we surrender what was always only an illusory ego and, no longer obstructed, enter the open arms of formless awareness. Finally, with the non-conceptual recognition of the ground of our being, the love of the higher for the lower and the love of the lower for the higher, so to speak, meet in embrace. We begin to realize the ever-present interpenetration of love by love—form and formlessness in thorough, complete, all-encompassing embrace. As the Indian sage, Nisargadatta, observes, the heart crosses the abyss that the mind creates.

We come, gradually, with love's intention, to see that this form, this self we mistook for the final statement on our being, is here as function. Once we change the nature of our relationship with each moment to that of an awakened stance, formlessness can function through form and spirit can shine through our transformed, utterly unique self.

We begin, gradually, to rest in the heart, the zero point between form and formlessness. We begin to live at the zero point, where the horizontal axis of the fabricated story of our egoic self meets the vertical axis of sacred presence in every moment, every new now. Thomas

# With that revelation of Presence, we surrender what was always only an illusory ego and…enter the open arms of formless awareness.

Keating regards the spiritual journey as a process of dismantling the monumental illusion that God is distant or absent. Aligned at the zero point, entered through the heart's contemplative eye, we come gradually to know sacred presence, in every moment and with every breath.

At the zero point of the heart, we add nothing to any arising experience—neither grasping nor embroidering with any narrative of self. And we subtract nothing from any arising experience—pushing nothing away nor wishing for other than what is. We welcome and we let go. "Just this" responds to each arising, adding nothing. "This, too" responds to each arising, subtracting nothing.

As WE BEGIN to abide more stably at this zero point, in the soul that mediates between self and spirit, higher-order capacities emerge in us. These are the fruits of transforming realizations. Beatitudes, the "noble qualities" of Buddhist practice, emerge when we have met formless presence and begin to abide more stably within it. The evidence is abundant.

Attachment gives way to appreciation. Politeness upgrades to kindness. Honor upgrades to integrity. Believing gives way to awe. Hope gives way to plenitude. Self-consciousness melts in the intimacy of self-forgetfulness. Unworthiness ceases in grateful humility. Judgment gives way to discernment. Confusion upgrades to clarity. Separation begins to dissolve in a growing experience of unity. Contraction in self eases into vastness, saturated with being. Conceptuality gives way to wisdom. Striving relaxes into awareness. Seeking reveals refuge. Defendedness melts into compassion.

Here replaces there. Now replaces then.

And love begins to flow. An insight widely attributed to Meister Eckhart notes that "What a person takes in by contemplation, that [s/he] pours out in love." The greatest fruit of our spiritual ripening is love. Returning to the love from which only our ignorance kept us, we begin to embody it. We begin to live in the world with an increasingly inclusive caring. We begin to live Christ's injunction to "love one another" and we unfold, finally, into the *Buddhas*—awakened beings—Christ wishes us to be.

With the eye of spirit, we finally open and fully use the precious gift of this human life. The realizations of the contemplative eye begin to transform the entire being. They transform the other two eyes so that they no longer operate in unconscious confusion, no longer view only separation and presumption. The eye of the senses begins to see the living dynamic of interbeing with clarity, wonder, and deep gratitude. The eye of intellect, involved in the creation of the world in every moment, begins to spontaneously act with greater care and deeper reverence. It begins to function in service to compassion, love, and justice, which Martin Luther King, Jr., noted is how love manifests in the public sphere.

Formed by love, we are born anew. Fueled by love, we search for the love that is searching. Through the contemplative eye, we find the love that we have always already been. The evidence of love is a full circle, a beautiful symmetry, Alpha and Omega. •

# Finding Spiritual Evidence Within the Self-Evident

*By Robert Sardello*

*"The Real Prayers Are Not the Words, but the Attention that Comes First"*
—Mary Oliver

## I.  EXITING THE AGE OF DOUBT

D IRECT, IMMEDIATE SPIRITUAL experience, self-evident spiritual experience, requires going through a process of subtraction from, rather than addition to, who we are and think we are. Culturally, we are on the cusp of a "great subtraction," one that can be seen not as loss but as the beginning of an "Age of Trust in the Incarnation." When we can be more present to the exciting sense of what is coming to be, rather than filled with fear at so much breakdown, we can feel the inner warmth of the longing for Divine presence.

Once the embers of longing for the Divine begin to warm, there is no place else to begin the search for true, immediate spiritual experience than from within our usual, culture-bound lens of awareness. Our present time might well be termed the ending of the "Age of Doubt." Religion, rituals, sermons, reading, going to workshops, conversations, study, and groups can assist in moving toward an inner transformation, but our culture of science and the practical technologies that emerge from the sequence of doubt-theory-hypothesis-test-evidence-application is founded on doubt. Scientific attitude permeates even individual experience. We are removed from direct experience—and don't even know that is the case. And, being removed from direct experience, the soul too lives in confusion.

We seem to sense the world, others, and ourselves with a kind of immediacy, but we live within the habit of a cultural consciousness, long established, of separating ourselves from others, the earth, the world—and the Divine. We seem to be "here," and all else seems to be "there," "other," and essentially unknown except when investigated, which does not yield direct "knowing," but only the removed form of "knowing about." This habit is so strong it also permeates our inner life. The immediacy of spiritual presences are removed from our ordinary means of awareness—ego-awareness—which cannot find the ever-present solace of being within and surrounded by the Divine Sensorium. The great contemplative traditions, with much practice, devotion, and dedication, can result in unitive awareness but, generally, such awareness is not supported in the world of daily living.

# Trust is an all-encompassing Presence, which requires our attention to open its creative activity.

There are indications that this culture is in transition. Openings occur, but so does exaggerated holding on to known ways. The separative culture is the culture of practical realism. It excludes what cannot be directly observed, verified, and used. These transitional times reveal themselves as a modification of this realism, which emphasizes the "value" of this worldview for the satisfaction of personal comfort and makes available "products" that would seem to satisfy every need, all the while obscuring the ability to see how this outlook is harming Earth. I call this modification of practical realism "practical me-ilism."

The achievements of the Age of Doubt rely on the exclusion of the "middle." Abstract cognition couples with intensification of the will, while the middle region of the heart is excluded as an actual world-forming capacity. As the Age of Doubt becomes shaky, an opportunity exists to notice what has been waiting here all along: the heart as the spiritual/physical organ capable of originating a world that is the true exemplification of the Incarnation. The evidence of this possibility requires developing heart-attention to the self-evident.

## II.  THE GREAT SUBTRACTION PROCESS OF TRUST

ATTENTION IS EVERYTHING. We are our attention. The achievements of the Age of Doubt rely on the capturing of attention. We see it everywhere. Something outside of our very being is continually put forth as satisfying unknown inner longings. We no longer trust what can be immediately, bodily felt as inwardly soul-present.

Noticing what is already spiritually present requires the capacity of free forces of attention. In the absence of such freedom it is as if life itself has become an "add on"—as if getting or having some product, some credential, or some training will bring all the satisfaction longed for. As the Age of Doubt crumbles, a most extraordinary and yet very simple presence also becomes more directly available: Trust, where we each, individually, in union with one another, can begin to notice that the spiritual worlds are here, all around and within us. We do not need to add anything to who we are to qualify for reception. We only need to notice the presence of Trust.

It is not that "I trust," nor is it that "I trust in you, or in someone or something"; it is the pure existence of Trust as an inherent force of the soul. We rely on it every moment. We could not walk from here to the front door without being immersed in bodily Trust. We could not see, hear, touch, taste, feel, think, or will—except for the already-available presence of Trust.

Opening awareness to the presence of Trust: I call this the "Living Prayer of Trust." Whatever you want, need, or long for, let your attention permeate your bodily being in such a way that you feel the presence of what seems to be missing.

When we pray it is usually for something that we do not have. It is a strange way to pray, for our attention is then removed from the fullness of what is already present and we only attend to what is not here, hoping that our prayers will be answered—when they are in fact already answered.

For example, I have been suffering for some months with plantar fasciitis, a painful malady of the bridge and heel of the foot. I allow and open to the body-feeling of what it is like to walk without pain. It is as simple as that—with attention, noticing the body as already healed, and feeling it. As I do so, I can actually feel that the spiritual gift of fullness of body is indeed present. I do not rely solely on some external thing to take the illness away. I still do accept the help of external medication, but I never lose the immediate fact that fullness of being is bodily already here.

Without this Trust, dulling, deadening, and medicating would be mistaken for a return to wholeness. This bodily sensing of the presence of Trust then builds the strength of a soul power, the inherent power of Trust—which begins to be experienced as everywhere and always present. Trust is an all-encompassing Presence, which requires our attention to open its creative activity. The daily prayer of Trust opens what is beyond doubt.

# What we feel within the heart is the ever-present holy sacredness, the spiritual nature of all that is present.

## III. THE EVIDENCE OF TRUST IS WITHIN
## THE SILENCE OF THE HEART

C HRIST DOES NOT "come and go," a ridiculous notion once Trust can be felt. Christ is present—always—and can be noticed, not with the mind or with the will of wanting this truth to be so, but with the attention of the heart. Trust is whole and opens up the whole of the Whole, centered in the heart.

Evidence is always related to the nature of what is being observed. We cannot expect to apply the "rules of evidence" from the Age of Doubt to the Age of Trust. New rules are needed. The Age of Trust is very individual, but no longer egotistically individual—individual-ism. Evidence of the presence of the spiritual worlds is always individual in character but general in resonance. I may not experience the exact content of spiritual presence as that which is bodily felt by another, but can feel the resonance when I am receptively open to another's description of spiritual experience. This active receptivity characterizes the very nature of the receptive Silence of the heart.

Here is one way to open to the receptive Silence of the heart:

Silence never leaves; we leave the Silence. She is the creative matrix of the soul-presence of everything—everything in the world. Silence has nothing to do with the absence of sound. It is a palpable presence. We experience Silence most easily within the natural world—walk into the redwood forests of California and Silence is thick. So it is in most natural places. To notice it daily, we have to learn how to notice. Sit quietly with eyes closed. Place your attention somewhere at the periphery of your body—your leg, for example. Attention is different than thought and it is different than "paying attention." It is an actual force that is subtle, but very real. Feel the bodily difference. Begin by paying attention to your big toe—it is as if "you" are "here" and your big toe is "over there." Then, place your attention within your big toe. You bodily feel as if you are "seeing" the world from the viewpoint of the "big toe."

Enter into the Silence by placing attention at a place at the periphery of the body for a few moments, noticing the feeling, and then directing attention to another place at the periphery of the body and again noticing. You will feel as if you are being lightly touched. That is the Silence. Then pour your attention into that quality of feeling lightly touched—and you are within the Silence. You will find it hard to leave.

Enter the Silence of the heart: After you have stayed for a while within the Silence, place your attention within the center of the heart—your actual heart—which is also simultaneously the spiritual heart. What is it like being within the heart? It is the realm of pure feeling—not feeling "this" or "that," but pure feeling—where it feels as if we are actually touching the Divine World. Feeling is like touching…when we feel something through immediate touch. What we feel within the heart is the ever-present holy sacredness, the spiritual nature of all that is present. You will not want to leave. Explore inwardly this invisible, unending, spherical, intimate, infinite, unbounded feeling-presence. Then, within the heart, silently, with your lips, gesture the word Christ. Let your attention notice the felt presence of Christ. Refrain from thinking and from interpretation. Remain within the Silence. In a short time it becomes possible, any place, any time, to shift attention into the Silence of the heart and be within the felt presence of the Divine nature that is simultaneously within you and within everything around you.

## IV. "YES, BUT I CANNOT FEEL THESE DIMENSIONS"

IT IS SO; in order to notice Trust, Silence, and heart presence, we have to have a "full deck of cards." The Age of Doubt has installed fear as the great separator. Fear cuts off, shuts down the other great feeling center of the body—the solar plexus.

This is the feminine center—the solar plexus, the inner sun, and the bodily experience of the Silence of Soul. The solar plexus is the region where the twelve nerves of the autonomic nervous system converge: the sun at the center of the internal zodiac. The solar plexus keeps all of the systems of the body—we could say "keeps all of Incarnation"—in harmony. Fear shuts down solar plexus awareness and, at the same time, inner-body harmony remains disturbed—felt as ever-present anxiety.

Establish the connection between heart and solar plexus: Imagine the solar plexus as the inner, bodily resonance of Mary/Sophia. Heart radiates love; solar plexus holds this love in active receptivity and giving. Opening the solar plexus is very easy. Begin always with entering into Trust, then the Silence, and then within the Silence of the heart. Then enter into solar-plexus awareness:

- Slowly take three deep breaths. Hold the fourth breath. Instead of exhaling, gently press down, feeling the area of the ribs expanding. Hold for a couple of moments. Slowly exhale, feeling the moving in of the rib area, the area of the solar plexus, which is right in back of the upper stomach. Do this breathing three times. This awakens the solar plexus so that we are within the wholeness of body, including all the so-called "unconscious" body processes. It is easy to feel the solar plexus—quite suddenly we feel the inner dimensionality of the body as sacred space. We realize that we have been living in our body as if it were a cardboard cutout.

- Let attention move to the solar plexus. Let the solar plexus open to utter stillness by gesturing, by silently moving the lips, and saying the word "Mary." Mary-presence is felt as the utter stillness of the solar plexus. Feel the solar plexus becoming completely calm.

We cannot go directly to the question of spiritual evidence without providing a way to be present to experiences that can then be verified—always individually—in resonance not only with the experiences of others but also with the Great Contemplative Tradition.

It is as if we have not fully realized that the Incarnation is about our incarnating, our becoming spiritual human beings rather than human beings who do spiritual things now and then.

I invite you to try each of the above—I will not call them "practices," but rather "prayers" of the Age of Trust in the Incarnation. •

# Intimations of Immortality

*The Oxford Book of English Verse*

Our birth is but a sleep and a forgetting:
The Soul that rises with us, our life's Star,
Hath had elsewhere its setting,
And cometh from afar:
Not in entire forgetfulness,
And not in utter nakedness,
But trailing clouds of glory do we come
From God, who is our home:
Heaven lies about us in our infancy!

At length the Man perceives it die away,
And fade into the light of common day.

Those shadowy recollections,
Which, be they what they may,
Are yet the fountain-light of all our day,
Are yet a master-light of all our seeing;
Uphold us, cherish, and have power to make
Our noisy years seem moments in the being
Of the eternal Silence: truths that wake,
To perish never:
Which neither listlessness, nor mad endeavour,
Nor Man nor Boy,

Nor all that is at enmity with joy,
Can utterly abolish or destroy!
Hence in a season of calm weather
Though inland far we be,
Our souls have sight of that immortal sea
Which brought us hither,
Can in a moment travel thither,
And see the children sport upon the shore,
And hear the mighty waters rolling evermore.

Thanks to the human heart by which we live,
Thanks to its tenderness, its joys, and fears,
To me the meanest flower that blows can give
Thoughts that do often lie too deep for tears.


–William Wordsworth (1770–1850)

# NOTES

## Editor's Note

1 *Portrait of a Radical: The Jesus Movement*, DVD. Produced and directed by DJ Kadagian (Ridgefield, CT: Four Seasons Productions, 2000).

2 Eugene H. Peterson, *The Message: The Bible in Contemporary Language* (Colorado Springs: NavPress, numbered edition, 2005).

## Evidential Mysticism and the Future of Earth

1 Carl Sagan, *Pale Blue Dot: A Vision of the Human Future in Space* (New York: Random House Publishing, 1994), 50.

2 Loyal Rue, *Everybody's Story: Wising Up to the Epic of Evolution* (Albany: SUNY Press, 2000), 42–43.

3 http://en.wikipedia.org/wiki/Big_History_Project, https://www.bighistoryproject.com/portal.

4 This portion originally published as Michael Dowd, "Is Scientific Evidence Modern-Day Scripture?" *The Huffington Post*, March 2, 2012, http://www.huffingtonpost.com/rev-michael-dowd/science-as-modern-scripture_b_1300193.html.

5 Loyal Rue, *Religion Is Not About God* (Piscataway, NJ: Rutgers University Press, 2005), 135.

6 Richard N. Ostling, "The Search for the Historical Adam," *Christianity Today* 55, no. 6 (2011).

7 Karl W. Giberson and Francis S. Collins, *The Language of Science and Faith: Straight Answers to Genuine Questions* (Downers Grove, IL: InterVarsity Press, 2011), 208.

8 http://youtube/DDMOF7qtlh8.

9 Michael Dowd, *Thank God for Evolution: How the Marriage of Science and Religion Will Transform Your Life and Our World* (New York: Penguin Group, 2009), 98.

### The Perils of Spiritual Faith, Doubt, and Evidence

1 Very generally, the contemporary canons of reason/rationality collapse the terms "evidence" and "proof," making them synonymous in meaning the need for either material evidence or logical proof (given to inferences) in order to hold a justified true belief—the "gold standard" of classical epistemology—in a certain state of affairs. Under such a canon, the state of affairs that "God exists" can be held to be true if certain conditions are met, depending on whether one is applying a deductive, inductive, or empirical form of reasoning. Deductively, for example, that God exists can be held to be true if the premises are true and linked to the conclusion such that the conclusion reached is necessarily true by the inferences of the premises.

2 So as not to confuse the reader, I am using the term "fabulation" as synonymous with "narrative reasoning." In the prior paragraph, I claim that faith needs reasons. However, these are not discursive reasons. The notion of narrative reasoning is found in the later works of Paul Ricœur. Our ability to tell stories is quite unique in that we can fit a colossal number of events into a plot that conveys meaning. The construction of a story does not follow a logical sequence based on inference. Rather, a story is order, drawn out of the cacophony of events, such that there is a beginning, a middle, and an end where, in the telling and listening, a new meaning arises. As it has over the centuries, the meaning arising from stories and myths can move a person in a way that a logical argument cannot.

3 Norman P. Tanner, ed., *Decrees of the Ecumenical Councils*, Vol. 2 (Washington, DC: Georgetown University Press, 1990), 810. This statement in isolation has been misinterpreted by clergy and the church hierarchy alike. For a nuanced reading see Fergus Kerr, "Knowing God by Reason Alone: What Vatican I Never Said," *Blackfriars*, 9 (2010): 213–359. Kerr makes the point that, despite the misinterpretation, the language of certainty, reason, and knowability finds its way into the contemporary *Catechism of the Catholic Church*, specifically Chapter 1, §31–§39. The role of dogma and tradition is to temper the excesses that might arise from, for example, the Reformation's position *of sola scriptura*, where one interpretation of Scriptures is pitted against another, leading to inevitable schisms. However, holding to any dogmatic position seduces one into providing the "best" justification and evidence for holding one interpretation over another. Whether any dogma can be defended except through political power is a separate discussion.

4 Christopher C. H. Cook, "Addiction and Spirituality," *Addiction*, 99 (2004): 539–55; for a more complete discussion, see Christopher D. Ringwald, *The Soul of Recovery: Uncovering the Spiritual Dimension in the Treatment of Addictions* (New York: Oxford University Press, 2002).

## Notes on Mystical Evidence

1 Thomas Merton, *Contemplative Prayer* (New York: Doubleday & Company, 1971), 38–39.

2 William Johnston, ed., *The Cloud of Unknowing* (New York: Image Books, Doubleday & Company, 1973), 46.

3 *A Thomas Merton Reader*, ed. Thomas P. McDonnell (New York: Image Books, Doubleday & Company, 1974), 504.

4 *The Collected Works of St. John of the Cross*, trans. Kieran Kavanaugh and Otilio Rodriguez (Washington, DC: ICS Publications, 1979), 141.

## Seeing with the Eye of the Heart

1 Kabir Helminski, *Living Presence: A Sufi Guide to Mindfulness and the Essential Self* (New York: Tarcher/Putnam, 1992), 157.

2 This is why the great mystics have always insisted (in the words of the fourteenth-century spiritual classic *The Cloud of Unknowing*) that "God may be reached and held close by means of love, but by means of thought never." *The Cloud of Unknowing*, ed. Ira Progoff (New York: Bantam Doubleday, 1957), 72.

## Transcendent Faith, Transcendent Art in the Rothko Chapel

1 http://www.fandor.com/films/the_rothko_chapel.

## Curing and Healing

1 John Polkinghorne, *Science and Religion in Quest of Truth* (New Haven: Yale University Press, 2011); John Polkinghorne, *One World: The Interaction of Science and Theology* (West Conshohocken, PA: Templeton Press, 2007).

2 Monika Hellwig, *Whose Experience Counts in Theological Reflection* (Milwaukee: Marquette University Press, 1982), 10–12.

3 L. William Countryman, *Living on the Border of the Holy: Renewing the Priesthood of All* (Harrisburg: Morehouse Publishing, 1999), 175.

4 Edmund D. Pellegrino, *The Philosophy of Medicine Reborn: A Pellegrino Reader* (Notre Dame: University of Notre Dame, 2008), 164; Craig Nelson, "The Familiar Foundation and the Fuller Sense: Ethics Consultation and Narrative," *The Permanente Journal*, 2012 Spring, 16(2):60–63.

5 Martin Buber, *I and Thou*, trans. Walter Kaufmann (New York: Charles Scribner's Sons, 1970 edition).

6 Viktor Frankl, *Man's Search for Meaning* (Boston: Beacon Press, 2006 edition), 121.

7 Jean Vanier, *Community & Growth: Our Pilgrimage Together* (New York: Paulist Press, 1979), 55–56.

Center for
Action and
Contemplation

A collision of opposites forms the cross of Christ.
One leads downward preferring the truth of the humble.
The other moves leftward against the grain.
But all are wrapped safely inside a hidden harmony:
One world, God's cosmos, a benevolent universe.